D1553645

Hitler's Jewish Olympian

FOILED
Hitler's Jewish Olympian

The Helene Mayer Story

Milly Mogulof

RDR Books
Oakland, California

RDR Books
4456 Piedmont
Oakland, CA 94611
Phone: (510) 595-0595
Fax: (510) 595-0598
E-mail: read@rdrbooks.com
Website: www.rdrbooks.com

ISBN 1-57143-092-X

Library of Congress Control Number 2002110527

Editor: Kim Klescewski
Associate Editor: Bob Drews
Text Design and Typography: Richard Harris
Cover Photo: © 1935 by Imogen Cunningham

Distributed in Europe by Airlift Book Company,
8 The Arena, Mollison Avenue, Enfield,
Middlesex, England EN37NJ

Printed in Canada

Contents

"To tell the truth
as much as human frailty permits. . . ."

—*George Seldes*
American journalist

An intensely focused young fencer,
Helene Mayer in training for championship matches

Chapter 1

THE GOLDEN "HE"

THE TIME IS AUGUST 1928. A beautiful, buoyant fencer not yet 18 years old represents Germany in the ninth Olympic Games of the modern era. Three thousand athletes and countless sports enthusiasts pour into Amsterdam, the host city. All are eagerly awaiting the events, aware of Germany's re-entry into the Games after eight years of exclusion. For Germany, the Games are of great consequence, a promising opportunity to restore its image after the horrors of World War I. A newly established democratic government, the Weimar Republic, seizes the opportunity to redeem itself as a chastised nation on the world scene and hopes it has found a hero in its beguiling contender for the gold medal in fencing.

Her name is Helene Mayer. A fencing prodigy at 13, she had captured the German senior championship in foil fencing in 1925, before her 15th birthday.[1] Going from victory to victory, Helene won championships in Germany and Europe, and the heart of the

1

German public. It was perhaps inevitable that she would catapult to Germany's Olympic fencing team in 1928. At the pinnacle of sports competition, her achievement was formidable for one so young and was a testament to her ambition, fortitude, and self-confidence. Helene was proud to represent her country in the Games.

A physically imposing athlete, Helene projected a powerful image at 5 feet, 10 inches tall and weighing 150 pounds. With a long torso, strong, graceful legs and the balance of a ballerina as she arched her body toward her opponent, she thrilled the German public. Under the wire face mask, her blue-eyed gaze was calm yet determined. Silky blonde hair wound around her ears, kept in place by a white headband stretched across her brow. Sometimes in the heat of competition, her hair tumbled down, evoking the unruly side of her nature. She was called the Golden "He," a shortened nickname for Helene (pronounced "Hay"), a name that captured the public's imagination. For a nation accustomed to more formality and conventional expressions, Golden "He" offered an uncommon intimacy with Germany's heroine.

Her noble bearing and sleek figure were heightened in dramatic photographs in newspapers and magazines throughout Germany. Journalists were lavish in their praise:

The whole world loves her! The most stark contrasts come together in a strangely unopposed way in this blonde girl—sinews and grace, energy and naiveté, gruffness and elegance.[2]

Helene's celebrity went well beyond her sport. There was belief in Germany that Helene was a German masterpiece and would invigorate her country's standing in the world.

Scheduled to be held in Berlin, the Olympic Games had come to a halt in 1916 in the throes of World War I. Germany, branded the aggressor in a war that claimed over 20 million lives, was excluded from the first two postwar Olympics, held in 1920 and 1924.

The International Fencing Federation allowed Germany into its fold in 1925. Italy, a country with great interest in fencing, was instrumental in getting Germany's membership approved, thus paving the way for participation in the 1928 Games.

Helene faced a golden opportunity in 1928 to help Germany return to the family of nations, and she did not let her country down. She fenced with surprising ease against opponents from Great Britain, Belgium, Holland, and against her German compatriot, Olga Oelkers, winning 18 matches and losing but two. The gold medal was hers! Queen Wilhelmina of Holland, a simple and unpretentious woman, looked like a pleased grandmother as she presented the prize to the respectful athlete.

Other German athletes performed admirably in 1928 as well. Carl von Langen-Parow won a gold medal in dressage. Gold medals went to a two-man team for rowing without a coxswain. Contenders in water polo and in weightlifting also received the highest award. German athletes won Olympic gold medals, but it was Helene who returned to Germany as a heroine, a celebrity, the *horerer tochter* or privileged daughter. She was the standard-bearer for the German nation. Her rewards included a private tea with President von Hindenburg, a medal awarding her the highest honors of the German State, and an unprecedented torch-lit parade in her hometown of Offenbach.

"The Helene Mayer cult no longer knew any boundaries. . . ."[3]

Inspired by images of the ancient Greek antecedents, white plaster-of-Paris figurines of Helene, dressed in her immaculate, form-fitting fencing costume, sold by the thousands all over Germany, prized possessions on mantelpieces everywhere. Helene embodied the German ideal of physical perfection, a flawless coming together of looks and performance. The German public felt a need to own a part of her. She made them feel good about themselves. To identify with Helene bolstered German self-esteem and national pride.

But trouble lurked. There was one significant fact about Helene's identity—just one dissonant detail that might stain her spotless image. Helene's father was Jewish.

Helene came of age during the most hospitable time for Jews in German history. Jewish settlement in Germany was permeated with dramatic cycles of acceptance and rejection. The granting of civil rights to Jews in 1871, when the German states united to form the empire, was a major step forward.[4] From that date the assimilation of Jews into German society accelerated. By 1910, the year Helene was born, Jews had a deepening sense of belonging. They embraced German civil life and culture. Helene was the daughter of Dr. Ludwig Mayer, a prominent German-born Jewish physician and athlete. Her mother was Christian. Intermarriage between Christians and Jews was increasing in Germany, and the Mayers felt at ease with their social status.

And yet there were rumblings and signs of danger. Although her looks were impeccably Teutonic, some considered her to be an oddity, an atypical German. They believed "Jewish blood" carried within it something tainted, unwholesome, and dangerous. They believed Jews to be eternal outsiders who could never measure up to German expectations of loyalty and patriotism. A person like Helene, no matter how outwardly attractive, presented a troubling image to those who believed in the purity of the German race. To them, Helene could never be the perfect exemplar of the German Volk, a mystical, all-encompassing concept of a people tied together by blood and an exclusively shared history. Jews were excluded from an essential and palpable *Deutschtum,* "German-ness." To the bigots, not only were Jews ineligible for membership in "the club," but they were also polluting the country.

Her Jewish background held little attraction or relevance to Helene. The painful history of the Jewish people in Germany was long since over. Helene could find little reason to identify with German-Jewish history and its forced expulsions, prejudice, and pogroms. Her ancestors could be viewed as helpless victims, timid and vulnerable in the face of greater powers. Perceived weakness was neither an attractive trait nor a palatable inheritance to a bold and self-assured athlete who had taken center stage.

Indeed, a friendly and generous atmosphere surrounded Helene in 1928. Optimism prevailed among those Germans who had faith in the eventual triumph of democratic rule. The economic outlook for Germany was improving, employment and the standard of living were rising, new buildings were under construction. German policies were creating trust in Europe and the United States. Membership in the League of Nations added increasing international stature. The duly-elected German parliament, the Reichstag, housed an array of political parties representing a wide spectrum of political beliefs.

But a unique political movement came into this scene, capturing the attention of cultist followers—the National Socialist

Party, also known as the Nazi Party, led by Adolf Hitler. Born in Austria in 1889, he drifted to Germany after serving in World War I. A spellbinding orator, Hitler attracted radical fringe groups and slowly gathered adherents into a small but dedicated cadre of followers. Founded in 1919, following Germany's ignominious defeat in the war, the Nazi Party saw Hitler, its seventh member, emerge as its visionary and propagandist.[5] He honed his demagogic skills in the raucous beer halls of Munich.

Party members opened their ears and pocketbooks to this man preaching fanatical nationalism and religious hatred. In 1920, the party program written by Hitler and his disciples declared that "only those of German blood, whatever their creed, may be members of the nation."

Initially, Hitler's extremism was ignored. He was scoffed at as a fanatical nobody who would soon disappear. Alliances among liberal and socialist parties would effectively deal with him, his party, his henchmen, and his war of words. His preachings of hate and contempt would be stifled as the country moved forward. The anti-Semites and the more virulent Nazis were not seen as a serious threat but as a small group of malcontents, envious of Jews and obsessively preoccupied by their improving status. After all, Jews were a mere 1 percent of the population, some 500,000 people out of a total population of about 50 million. In the halls of the Reichstag, anti-Nazi parties renounced the voices of repression and discrimination.

There was no cause for alarm among the democrats, the Jews, and the world community. Many journalists and political analysts declared the Nazis doomed in the wake of the 1928 elections when National Socialist candidates received 800,000 votes out of 31 million votes cast. They controlled only 12 parliamentary seats out of 491 in the Reichstag.[6] The party remained on the outer fringes of German political life.

For Helene, 1928 was a precious and defining time. She saw herself as a world-class athlete and a loyal citizen serving a benign and loving fatherland. The homage paid her reinforced her feelings of deep belonging and self-respect. Her admirers saw her as a youthful goddess, untarnished by scandal, shame, or scars of war. Like her supporters, she was willing to overlook her Jewish ancestry—no conflict, no contradictions.

Basking in the glow of her Olympic victory, she couldn't possibly have known that in just a few years time her Jewish link would become the ultimate test by which she was judged. Her father was born a Jew and would forever be identified as one. His blood was her blood. Her accomplishments and gifts to Germany would be dismissed and nullified because of it. In 1928, Helene's heritage was a fact. It would become a cruel fate.

1928 Olympic Torch Lighting Ceremony

Chapter 2

THE OLYMPICS BEFORE 1928

"THE OLD HELLENES WOULD HAVE TAKEN HELLENISTIC DELIGHT in this Helene, who embodied their ideal of mankind, of sport, beauty, and athletic talent."[1] This passionate quote, from a German newspaper during the 1928 Olympic Games, linked Helene directly to the ancient Greek games and found inspiration in the connection. Helene, meaning "light" in Greek, remained a favored name in European countries throughout the centuries and a testament to the persistent influence of Greek culture and sports. The young Helene had all the attributes of an ancient goddess.

The German public seemed to relish this pleasing tie to ancient Greece, where the Games started in 776 B.C. It was a simple affair consisting of a sprint for male-born citizens. Women were even forbidden from entering the sacred grounds at the foot of Mount Olympus.[2] As the Greek empire thrived and grew, so did the Olympic Games. And the role of women expanded—to presenting the crown of leaves to the victor.

The later Spartan rulers brought variety to successive Olympiads, introducing bloody wrestling matches and a series of three sequential events—running, jumping, and spear throwing. They included the discus throw as well. Roman invaders altered the scope and tone of the Games, adding boxing, where in vicious encounters competitors wrapped their fists in leather thongs, sometimes embedded with nails. Mutilation was a mark of honor and achievement.

For over 1,000 years the Games persisted, only to lose their vitality and importance as the Roman Empire faded and Christianity emerged. Theodosius, the first Christian emperor, considered the Games pagan and had them banned in 393 A.D.[3] An earthquake in the 6th century buried the ancient Greek arena.

Although abandoned for centuries, memories of the Olympics persisted. An idealized image of the ancient athlete, a noble mind in a noble body, was entrenched in human consciousness. At the close of the 19th century, a bold idea emerged. The resurrection of the Olympic Games fascinated a French nobleman, Pierre de Coubertin. In 1892, de Coubertin's vision and commitment to sport appealed to American and European enthusiasts at an international conference in Paris. He found support for renewal of the Games to be held every four years in great cities of the world. His somewhat naïve belief that revival of the Games "will bring Athleticism to a high state of perfection and a love of concord and respect for life"[4] overlooked the many tales of the ancient Games fraught with conflict and competition gone awry.

After almost four years of persuasion and planning, de Coubertin's dream came true. Participating nations would have the exciting opportunity to present their finest athletes on a world stage. In 1896, the first Olympic Games of the modern era were held in Athens, in deference to their great birthplace.

The Games were a huge success. True to ancient Greek tradition, Spiridon Loues won the highlight event, the marathon run. The modest Greek peasant stumbled into the arena after many grueling hours of running in the blazing summer heat. The two sons of King George of Greece leapt from the royal box to run alongside the first hero of the modern Olympic Games.[5] Forty years later, at the 1936 Olympics in Berlin, Loues presented a branch of an olive tree from an ancient grove on Mount Olympus to Adolf Hitler, chancellor of Germany.

The Games moved to Paris in 1900, where there was good news for female athletes. Golf and lawn tennis were allowed as unofficial events for women.

The United States hosted the 1904 Olympics in St. Louis, which featured a carnival-like display called "Anthropology Days" featuring "uncivilized tribes" including Native Americans, who competed against each other in pole vaulting, mud fighting, and a tug of war. But the idea of international competition had caught on, and commitment to the Games persisted.

The London Games of 1908 flourished, with new facilities— a track, swimming pool, and soccer fields. Women competed officially for the first time, with the addition of figure skating and yachting paving their way to further inclusion. Descriptions of inter-country disagreements were included in the first comprehensive report. Issues of overwrought nationalism arose. Russians tried to prevent Finns from displaying their flag. Some Englishmen objected to the Irish displaying their flag.

In Stockholm in 1912, advances in technical gadgetry were used. Electronic timing devices helped settle scoring issues. A new stadium was opened by King Gustav V, but the Swedes refused to allow boxing matches. A unilateral decision was made by the International Olympic Committee to limit the power of the host country in future Games.

Olympic heroes were emerging. Jim Thorpe, the "big Indian" from the United States and a gold medal winner, was hailed as the greatest athlete of the first half of the 20th century. Swimming and diving events for women were added. De Coubertin politely disagreed. "We feel the Olympic Games must be reserved for men: the solemn and periodic exaltation of athleticism with internationalism as a base and female applause as a reward."[6]

Helene was six years old when World War I caused cancellation of the 1916 Games. They resumed in 1920, 18 months after the armistice was signed in Antwerp, Belgium. Belgium was awarded the Games in recognition of the destruction inflicted on that small country during the war. In 1920, the official Olympics flag, with five differently colored interlocking circles representing the five major land masses of the world, was introduced. The Olympic oath, "We swear that we will take part in the Olympic Games in loyal competition, respecting the regulations which govern them in the true spirit of sportsmanship for the honor of our country and for the glory of sport," was spoken by athletes for the first time.

Several American athletes recalled in their memoirs the physical discomfort they endured in Antwerp after an equally uncomfortable two-week ocean voyage on an antiquated ship carrying them across the Atlantic. Their Olympic "village" consisted of bare and uninviting rooms in a converted schoolhouse furnished with straw pillows and narrow cots.

Germany and its World War I allies, Bulgaria, Hungary, Turkey, and Austria were excluded from the 1920 Olympic Games. At the time Helene was 10 and beginning her career as a talented, ambitious fencer. Would Germany be allowed to re-enter the Olympics four years hence? Helene was among the hopefuls, but Germany's exclusion was extended to the 1924 Games held in Paris.

The 1924 Games were in stark contrast to the dismal 1900 Paris event. These Games were well-run and professional, and they received worldwide attention. Over 3,000 athletes from 44 countries participated. A new competition was foil fencing.

During those years, Helene established her reputation. She had won the German youth fencing championship in 1923 at the age of 13 and was the youngest contender ever. In 1928, she was poised for international stardom. Her dream was about to be realized.

The official inclusion of foil fencing in 1924 was further acknowledgment of the role of women athletes in Olympic competition. In 1928 they were allowed to participate in track and field events—running, jumping, discus, javelin, and shot put—competitions that had previously been denied them as too masculine.

By 1928, the Olympic Games were a world phenomenon. The sporting events fed the public's appetite for grander and grander presentations. Countries had to find resources to pay the growing costs. Citizens traveled more comfortably, cheaply, and conveniently as transportation improved. Thousands of spectators filled the stadiums, cheering the world's best athletes and reserving their loudest ovations for their own country's contenders. Improved scoring devices, public address systems, and photographic enhancements heightened interest and fairness. Radio and newspaper coverage added to the sense of celebration and excitement. The 1928 Games "provided the first hint of the specialized corporate style management that would come to typify games of the future."[7] The U.S. track team had a manager and a staff of 20 to assist the athletes.

Relationships between sports and politics, nationalism and internationalism, athlete and country were becoming more complicated. Germany's exclusion from the 1920 and 1924 Games was a powerful stigma so that in 1928 its athletes felt they had something to prove to the world community.

The forces of democracy seemed to be in the ascendancy, reflecting Olympic ideals. The Games were to serve as a force for peace and reconciliation, and yet because athletes represented their country, it almost ensured that nationalistic interests would remain paramount. As the Games became politicized, the role of the athletes changed as well. The hope was to preserve a delicate balance between expressions of national pride and blatant excesses of superiority and desire to prevail.

It was in this context that Helene would compete. Participants in the Games were at the same time world-class athletes, fierce competitors, and citizens of a nation. In 1928, a jubilant Germany, intent on rehabilitating its reputation, had in Helene an athlete who was a superb master of her sport and also an adored national representative of Germany.

Helene, as was true of many other German Jews, knew little of the continuing Jewish experience in Germany. To Helene, the past was faded and she lived in a sparkling present. But to understand Helene's story it is vital to understand the history of her Jewish ancestry and the Mayer family as they emerged and prospered. Helene brought her own uniqueness to the story. She was the first person in the Mayer family to become a famous athlete, the first to receive national acclaim. Her Jewish heritage would have a profound effect on her future, both as an athlete and as a German.

A rare photo of Helene and her parents,
Dr. Ludwig Mayer and Ida Mayer

Chapter 3

THE JEWISH LEGACY

THE MIGHTY RHINE RIVER, flowing north to south in a land that was to become Germany, sheltered the first settlement of Jews as they made their way west across Europe. The river provided a fertile environment for the development of agriculture, industry, and trade.

As Germany developed a national identity, its people claimed a special bond with the river. Over many centuries, the Rhine came to represent a grandiose place of mythical power and purity. The Jews also had a claim to the rich Rhineland, but theirs was as the home to a small band of exiles who founded small communities on its banks. They put down roots slowly and painstakingly, earned their livelihoods, raised families, and attempted to practice their religion freely.

The story of Jewish settlement unfolded in the pre-Christian Era. After Roman troops destroyed Jerusalem in 70 A.D., wandering bands of Jews scattered to different parts of the world. Eventually, some found themselves in the Rhineland. By the 3rd century, merchants, wine growers, artisans, and an occasional physician had become part of that Jewish community.[1] As the expanding Christian church assumed religious and temporal powers, pagan Roman beliefs faded, supplanted by Christian doctrine. During the first 700 years of settlement in the Rhineland, relative peace and prosperity prevailed between the Jews and their host communities.

The Jews, with different language, customs, and religion, were a minority in the midst of a dominant Christianized population that settled in emerging towns along the Rhine. The town of Mainz was home to one of the oldest Jewish communities.[2] Many centuries later, it was the town where Helene Mayer's paternal family put down roots. In Mainz, the most ancient Jewish gravesites in Germany can be found, attesting to seven centuries of a continuing Jewish community.

Events in the town of Mainz reflected the ever-changing relationship with the Jews. As time passed, accommodations between the Jews and their neighbors were intermittently disturbed. Jews were often singled out, blamed, and punished for any unexpected calamities. In 1084 many left the town after being accused of setting a fire that caused extensive damage to their ghetto. A local bishop offered respite, inviting them to settle in the nearby town of Speyer, where, declared the bishop, they "would increase the luster of the city a thousand fold."[3]

In 1096 a series of attacks gained momentum. The Crusaders led focused assaults, demanding conversion to Christianity. As the invading Crusaders terrorized and plundered Jewish communities, they met tremendous resistance in Mainz. More than 1,000 Jews chose death rather than convert in what has come to be known as "the Mainz massacre."

In the early 13th century, Jews of Mainz were ordered to wear a distinguishing item exposing them as a marked and vulnerable minority. It could be a distinctive item of clothing, a hat, cloak, or footwear. The item, however differentiating, did not diminish mercantile activities. Mainz Jews developed commercial connections with Greece and Italy. Moneylending became increasingly important. Many churches and monasteries borrowed money from Jewish moneylenders, a prohibited activity for Christians.

In 1348, the Black Death, a deadly plague, brought ruin to Jewish inhabitants along the Rhine. Over half the population of Europe, 7.5 million people, succumbed. The Jews were targeted to explain the confounding epidemic. They were prey to hysterical accusations as carriers of filth and poisoners of wells.[4] The fact that the Jews themselves were also victims of the plague did not deter the irrational belief that somehow they were responsible for it.

In the mid-16th century there is evidence in an imperial police code that a generic, more obvious symbol of Jewish identity, was required. The yellow badge was selected as the symbol.

CONCERNING THE DRESS OF JEWS:

1. The Jews shall wear a yellow ring on their coats or caps wherever they go, unconcealed and publicly, so that they may be recognized.

2. In order that this regulation and statute concerning their clothing and ornaments may be more firmly observed and enforced, we require that when anyone has

transgressed and violated the law then he shall be punished with confiscation of the clothes or ornaments and
by a fine twice the value of the clothes or ornaments.[5]

The yellow badge would become the yellow star used to
identify and vilify the Jewish victims of the Nazi regime in the
20th century.

A cyclical pattern of inclusion and exclusion for Jews in
German lands was a way of life that lasted well into the modern
era. In good times, the Jewish community became more self-
assured and benefited from periods of rapid social change.
Liberating ideas about the rights of man slowly began to take
hold in Europe and had a startling effect on Jews as well as other
disenfranchised people. The revolutionary events in France in
the 18th century spread into Germany, where Jews were granted citizenship, the right to buy land, to settle wherever they
chose, the right to serve in the army, and to marry non-Jews.
(The rights to hold public office and to attend a German university were withheld.) Unfortunately these rights were short-
lived; by 1815 each German state was permitted to change its
position on the "Jewish Question" and the non-binding rights
were rescinded.

Emmanuel Mayer, Helene's great-grandfather, was born in
Mainz in 1810, her great-grandmother, Julie Weissman, in
1812.[6] A great debate on whether civil and political rights for
Jews would endure began in earnest during their childhoods.
Many Jews lived in two worlds at that time, the Jewish and the
German, but they began to feel inexorably drawn to the German
nation as it pulled itself together as an imperial country, unified
under a single emperor. As Jews were permitted to assimilate,

they were allowed to gradually divest themselves of the outward trappings that labeled them, the distinctive Jewish hat and the yellow badge.

In this environment, Julie Weissman and Emmanuel Mayer married. They lived in Mainz and raised a family. Martin Mayer, Helene's paternal grandfather, was born in 1841. Martin began life in a promising era. In 1848, a national assembly, held in Frankfurt, adopted a new constitution. One section, dealing with the fundamental rights of people living in Germany, stated that rights were not dependent on religious creed. The document reflected a liberalization of public opinion and politics. Bitter debates accompanied the attempts to confer citizen status on the Jews. Pressure arose from opposing groups for Jews to convert to Christianity.

The debate about the "Jewish Question" preoccupied many writers. In the last three decades of the 19th century, over 1,200 books, pamphlets, treatises, and essays were written about the nature and fate of the Jew.[7] Were the Jews only a religious group? Were they an alien people bent on infiltration into a pure German culture? A watchful anxiety prevailed as the Jews became more prosperous and demanded inclusion.

Most of these publications opposed the Jews. William Marr, a failed journalist who coined the term "anti-Semitic," warned in 1873 that with emancipation, Jews would control the economy.[8] If the process continued, he wrote, Germany would be ruined. The idea of being anti-Semitic—in opposition to the Jews—stuck in German consciousness. It began to represent a position of those who wanted to curb Jewish influence, to restrain Jews' civil rights.

By the mid-19th century, the Jewish population of Mainz

had grown to 3,000, almost 5 percent of the city. The community was large enough to support various congregations, from orthodox to more liberal forms of religious practices. The Jews had created a network of educational and social service institutions. The position of the Jews gradually improved educationally and economically. The narrative of the Jewish experience in Mainz told a dramatic story of the development of Jewish life in Germany. It was not an atypical German story.

Despite these gains, Germany's "Jewish Question" was unresolved. Jews' civil rights were withheld, delayed, rescinded, or grudgingly granted. Jews were at the mercy of the incipient nation as a particular kind of German consciousness took hold. Eternal outsiders to some, they were a people under surveillance and control. There was suspicion that in spite of their small numbers, the Jews caused untold harm: mysterious fires, the Black Death, refusal to convert to Christianity, unshakable myths of blood libel—drawing blood from a kidnapped Christian child to be used for ceremonial purposes.

The Jews managed to take advantage of the positive periods to improve their situation, build communities, and attach themselves to the liberal ideas of personal freedom and the rights of man. Acts of disheartening regression shared the stage with acts of tantalizing advances. A political seesaw kept the Jews in an uneasy state.

The assimilating Jew believed he could be a good Jew and a good German at the same time. Martin Mayer, Helene's grandfather, was such a man. He took advantage of a progressive cycle and during his long life rose to become an affluent and influential citizen of Mainz. A successful businessman and malt manufacturer, Mayer became increasingly active in the political and civic life of the city.

In 1871, the diverse patchwork of independent German states, each with its own laws, politics, and economic conditions, joined to form the German Empire. The granting of full civil rights to German Jews enabled Mayer's rise to prominence. The flowering of the Jewish community that began in 1871 took the Jews from the places where they had settled originally, in the Rhineland, to burgeoning urban centers all over Germany. They were free to move about, no longer confined to ghettoes along the river's banks. By 1871, the Jews had plentiful opportunities in business and the professions. Some 60 percent of them were members of the upper middle class; they felt a growing kinship with Germany, a part of the developing civic and cultural life. Despite these advances, emancipation was not without its problems. Discrimination persisted in admittance to the officer corps in the army, in the teaching professions, particularly with professorships, and the holding of high public office.

Martin Mayer may have been particularly talented or fortunate to have lived in Mainz, an embracing city that had moved forward with the times. In 1884, at the age of 43, "a loyal co-worker and dear colleague," Mayer became a town councilor and advisor to the mayor. It was not unusual for prominent Jews to be "advisors" to people in power. A newspaper article and obituary described him as one

> . . . who had long played an important role in the public, political and municipal life of Mainz. Martin Mayer was already active in politics as a young man and always in a libertarian democratic sense . . . he was co-founder of the Democratic Party—at various elections he fought side by side with the social democratic party.

The obituary continued:

On July 5th, he was elected honorary councilor to the mayor. He supervised the harbor and storage deputation, the museum deputation for the preservation of the Museum of Antiquities and the Museum of Natural History. He served on the board of the city orchestra, as well as involvement in matters of finance and taxation. We will always honor the memory of the deceased and the great joy he put into his work. He labored to promote the city's interest in a selfless manner.[9]

Martin Mayer, a man of drive, confidence, and accomplishment, felt himself to be a free and nearly full citizen of Germany. As a Jew, he had to settle for being councilor to the mayor rather than being the mayor himself. Affiliation with the Social Democratic Party was an obvious choice for him. For 20 years, from 1880 through 1900, the party fought continuing anti-Semitism.

Mayer's obituary did not mention his Jewish identity, his family life, or any affiliation with the Jewish community. It was solely concerned with his public service and political life. Perhaps his heritage went unmentioned because it was deemed irrelevant, or better left unsaid.

Mayer and his wife, Rosalie Hamburg, had fulfilling and honorable lives. For their three sons, Eugen, Ludwig, and George, and their daughter, Anna, the family would have expected continuing Jewish assimilation into the German nation, with intact civil rights ensuring a safe future.

Ludwig Karl Mayer, Helene's father, was born in March 1876.

Educational and professional opportunities were growing. Ludwig and his brothers could attend German universities. To an upper-class, self-confident German Jew, the future beckoned. Liberalism outweighed repression; Jews were being included, not excluded. If the German Jews remained vigilant and used rational, legal means to combat anti-Semitism, they would prevail, or so the belief went. The hope for the triumph of reason appeared to justify a Jew's belief in his rightful, earned place in German society. Accomplishments were rewarded and recognized.

Ludwig Mayer's talents and interests, inspired by his father's contributions, led him in new and promising directions. He decided to become a physician. As a doctor, community leader, sportsman, and father, his life was the epitome of success. His achievements expanded his world and that of his children, particularly Helene. Sports provided a distinct opportunity for Jews yearning for integration into all aspects of community. Ludwig and his wife, Ida, a former nurse, supported their daughter's talents although they could not possibly have foreseen that she would become a world-famous German fencer.

Women fencing circa 1900,
believed to have been taken at Mills College in Oakland, California,
where Helene Mayer eventually joined the faculty

Chapter 4

THE EARLY YEARS IN OFFENBACH–
BEGINNING THE JOURNEY

DR. MAYER FELT A DEEP CONNECTION to the city of his birth, Mainz, but settled in Offenbach am Main, a suburb of Frankfurt, in 1906, to practice medicine. Like his father, Ludwig became a beloved and prominent citizen. Helene was born there on December 10, 1910, the second of three children. She followed her brother Eugen by a year. The youngest child, Ludwig, was born five years after Helene, during World War I.

The birth certificates of the three children identified them as *Israelitischen,* or Jewish, their parents seemingly untroubled asserting this identity. Frau Mayer was Christian. She was a native of Silesia, on Germany's eastern border. Silesia's population was German-speaking, though it was claimed periodically by Prussia, Czechoslovakia, and eventually, Poland. Frau Mayer's father had been a well-known physician in Silesia.

Her marriage to a Jew was not unusual. By 1910, 13 percent of Jewish men and 10 percent of Jewish women married non-

Jews, nearly twice as many as in the prior decade.[1] In 1906, Dr. Mayer began private practice as a general practitioner in Offenbach after completing medical studies at universities in Heidelberg, Freiburg, Berlin, and Greiswald. He met Ida, a nurse who became his wife, during his training. After completing his medical apprenticeship, including time spent with a well-known professor in Frankfurt, he took up residence with his wife in Offenbach.

From the early 17th century on, most of Offenbach's Jews were refugees from Frankfurt. The Offenbach community resembled other German settlements, with a history of persecution and trauma followed by respites and reconciliation. The number of Jews remained constant at about 2,000, which amounted to about 3 percent of the population, throughout the 19th century and into the 20th.[2]

The Mayers were not practicing Jews, although Dr. Mayer, along with Rabbi Dienemann of Offenbach and other prominent Jews, were members of the Central Organization of German Citizens of Jewish Faith, the Centralverein. Founded in 1893 to combat anti-Semitism, the organization became the largest and most influential Jewish association in Germany. It grew to include half of the Jewish population, some 250,000 affiliated individuals, and had 500 local chapters. The major goals of the Centralverein were "strengthening Jewish self-confidence" and "the preservation of Judaism."[3]

Members were respected citizens, often allied with democratic and socialist political parties. They fought anti-Semitism through "persuasion with enlightening argument." As Jews prospered and grew bolder, a legal branch of the organization was established. Dozens of pamphlets were published "contradicting anti-

Semitism," and the Jews managed to boycott and rebuke newspapers like *Der Stuermer (The Attacker),* a particularly vicious anti-Semitic newspaper. Beginning in 1900, local branches had campaigned against anti-Semitic politicians. They became more outspoken in maintaining the retention of civil rights for Jews who, after all, cherished their historical and cultural heritage in a German context. Ludwig was a life-long member of the Centralverein.[4]

The Mayers settled into an orderly life. The couple began to raise a family in a comfortable home, not unlike Dr. Mayer's childhood home in Mainz. He quickly established a reputation as a dedicated physician. He was nicknamed *der Meenzer,* citizen of Mainz, a man who "was full of humor and had a splendid golden gruffness behind which he tried, but could not hide, a heart that was too soft."[5] He also was a fine athlete, a president of the Federal League of Sports, and served on sports club boards, promoting rowing and fencing. He was an outstanding diver who swam regularly throughout his life.

Dr. Mayer's love of sport was passed on to his children. Helene was encouraged in athletics. She had exceptional talent, a robust physique, and an eagerness to excel. Some believed Helene had taken up athletics because she was a fragile child, but the fragility was of short duration and due to severe food shortages during World War I. Helene was 4 when the war began and she recalled meals of watery soup and weak tea. In later years, she remembered that she had ravenously sucked marrow from bones to supplement a lean diet, a lifelong habit she never outgrew.[6] Helene also revealed that she suffered from curvature of the spine and was sent for physical therapy; part of the therapeutic regime was fencing.

Helene's athletic aptitude was prodigious. She excelled in

skiing, horseback riding, swimming, and dance. By age 7 she was a promising ballet student, appearing as a soloist in Offenbach in 1919. The balance, grace, and stamina that were required in ballet proved perfect qualifications for a fencer. Her father played an important role in encouraging and fostering his young daughter's ultimate athletic choice.

Why fencing, an elegant and aristocratic sport? It was a sport that conveyed high rank and a superior place in society. Fencing evolved as a sport in the mid-19th century, although swordsmanship, as a pastime and mode of warfare, was practiced by many ancient civilizations—Persians, Greeks, Romans—as well as German tribes. In the 14th century, as swords became lighter and more manageable, skill, rather than brute strength, became of paramount importance. By the 15th century, European guilds of fencing masters developed jealously guarded, secret strokes and sold them to combatants, making the surprise thrust an effective means of overcoming an opponent.

The Italian masters were the first to use the point of the sword rather than the edge. The lighter sword was called a "foil" because its point was flattened or "foiled" and then padded to reduce bodily harm. The adoption of the foil resulted in more subtle hand and footwork. Change spread throughout Europe with new emphasis on intelligence, speed, and strategy.[7] When the lunge—a forward thrust of the body—came into practice, the look of fencing was forever changed. Fencing became an athletic art form, and foil fencing became increasingly stylized. The fencers were capable of performing attacking and defensive movements using only one arm and hand. These changes encouraged female contenders, who could handle the lighter foils and execute nimble footwork.

After the Renaissance, dueling as an accepted means of settling disputes lost favor. The earlier duels were slowly replaced by the establishment of sporting events with clearly defined rules of engagement, leading to victory or defeat without serious injury. (It is interesting to note that Schlager fencing—using a long, cutting weapon—was in vogue and remained popular in Germany until World War II. Only blows aimed at cheeks were allowed.)[8]

At the end of the 18th century, a face mask was added, thereby minimizing the risk of eye injuries and facial wounds that had resulted from swift hits at close range. The complex "phrases," or exchange of blows, required strict rules. Fencing with foils became a "conversation of blades," a taming of the sport to avoid mutilation. With her natural talent and training in ballet, Helene was a perfect candidate to take advantage of the transformation in fencing.

Fencing demands quick thinking, poise, balance, and muscular control. With its reliance on strategy and tactics to outwit the opponent, it has been likened to a chess game played at lightening speed. The sport has a long tradition of informal bouts between men and women; competitors meet as equals, separated by ability alone. Fencing between men, in the past often a means of mortal, bloody combat, offered an enticing, growing arena for women athletes. Swordsmanship gave way to a gentler, more refined exchange.

In universities and fencing clubs throughout Germany, Austria, and other European countries, fencing was closed to Jews. Despite the barriers, fencing appealed to Jews for the same reason it appealed to all of those who embraced its steely nobility. With the influx of Jewish students to German universities during the late 19th and 20th centuries, its popularity grew.

Since fencing societies and fraternities listed religious affiliation next to each name on their club rosters, Jews formed their own clubs. Fencing provided an exclusive environment to challenge notions of Jewish weakness and timidity.

In 1886, a group of Jewish students in Breslau organized a fencing club to defend "Jewish honor" by challenging anti-Semitic students to duels. The invitations offended their opponents, who questioned the audacity of Jews to act as equals. Dueling had enormous appeal to the young and daring students who, with hotheaded gusto, proclaimed, "no one injures me with impunity."[9] In Berlin, a Jewish group organized a dueling fraternity in 1894. Their colors were white, black, and yellow. Yellow was chosen particularly as a reminder of when Jews had to wear the distinguishing yellow circle. "What was once a mark of shame became a mark of honor and a memorial to the guilt of our enemies" were the words of the club song.[10]

Dueling became a way for upper-class Jews to combat anti-Semitism and express their rage in a carefully controlled setting. At that time in Germany, many Jews served in the German army, where dueling was an expected skill. It was likely that Helene's father, on his path to assimilation, was attracted to fencing during his university days. The university that he attended in Freiburg had active fencing clubs. Dr. Mayer's eldest son, Eugen, followed his father's athletic bent and became an accomplished amateur fencer. He often complained that it was more difficult to prove himself because of his sister's fame. The young Helene partnered with her brother, and throughout her career coveted matches with the opposite sex. Ludwig, the younger brother, preferred soccer, to the dismay of his mother since he was always in a disheveled state.

The rules of engagement were firmly in place at the time Helene began to fence. In a series of advances and retreats, the object was to score a touch on your opponent before he or she scored one on you. The fencer gripped the handle of the foil. All foils have a light, flexible steel blade, a guard, a handle, and a pommel, an end.

The fencers meet on "the strip," a delineated area 46 feet long and 6½ feet wide. At the commencement of a bout the fencers stand at attention in the "on guard" position, a prescribed stance, so far apart as to require a lunge to reach the opponent. They then salute the judges and each other. When the referee orders "Fence!" the duel begins.

The on-guard position is the most important fencing fundamental, insuring balance and mobility. Three basic sequential movements follow: a "lunge"—the extension of the foil and the body toward a hit, a "parry"—a defensive action that deflects the attackers foil, and a "riposte"—a comeback attack that follows a successful parry. The attacker is said to have the "right of way." The contestant who is attacked must defend himself—parry—before assuming the offensive action—riposte. When both fencers are hit simultaneously, judges award the touch to the one with the right of way. Fencers score using the point of the foil, touching the opponent on the torso only. If the head, legs, or arms are touched, no point is scored.

The complexities of foil fencing with its established rules of engagement evolved over hundreds of years. So too with the scoring procedures. The number of minutes allowed for a typical bout (individual contests), the number of rounds in a bout, the number of hits required to win a bout, all underwent many modifications. (The first appearance of electronic scoring to aid referees in the task of making correct judgments was operative in the Berlin Games in 1936. Apparently, the new device was not used in the women's matches.) Currently, bouts have three 3-minute rounds, with a 1-minute break between each round. After each point, scored by a hit or a touch, the fencers return to their en garde position. The first fencer to reach 15 hits or touches in the course of the three rounds is the winner. (As of January 2002, rules are the same for both women and men. In the past this was not the case.)

A fencer wore a heavy mask, thick bib, jacket, and knickers. A padded glove completed the outfit. Towards the end of the 19th century, some fencers wore black uniforms, and foils tipped in white chalk were used to aid in the scoring. Gradually, following World War I, white canvas uniforms were introduced. Photographs of Helene in her fencing costumes highlighted her intense concentration and the perfection of her movements, particularly the remarkable lunge that seemed to traverse the entire fencing area.

Fencing was one of four sports included in each modern summer Olympic Games dating to 1896. Baron Pierre de Coubertin of France, the founder of the modern Games, was himself a fencer. The women's foil event was added in 1924 and was won by a Dane.

Offenbach was known as a center of German fencing and Helene received excellent training there.[11] Her entrance to fencing was inspired by Cavaliere Artur Gazzera, an Italian fencing master and highly acclaimed coach and gymnast who lived in Offenbach. He awakened a love of fencing in his eager 10-year-old student. Lunge, parry, and riposte were practiced daily in the Mayers' backyard at 6 a.m. before Helene began her school day. She continued with her ballet training as well. In 1923, at age 13, she performed an evening of dance in Offenbach. It was her farewell dance performance.[12]

Fencing won out. She won the German National Youth Championship that same year.

In 1924, she entered the German Senior Fencing Championship for the first time. Helene came in second, after her Offenbach teammate, Stephanie Stern. In 1925, Helene won the title and kept it for six years, a series of successes unequaled in Germany.

The conjoining of three influences in Helene's formative years brought her to a sport that became central to her persona. First was the hard work and inspiration of her instructor, Cavaliere Gazzera. Second was her father's encouragement and support of fencing, which had potent meanings to ambitious German Jews. And third was her aptitude and appetite for success.

Helene's Jewish identity was not hidden. A newspaper article describing her childhood stated: "In the neighborhood, Helene was called the 'Jewish Mayer' as opposed to the 'Christian Mayer'—a neighbor's child who lived next door in order to better distinguish the two. Indeed, it sometimes happened that curious journalists attempted to interview 'the wrong Mayer.'"[13] Why not call Helene the "athletic Mayer" rather than the "Jewish Mayer"? The reliance on ethnicity as a distinguishing characteristic had ominous implications for the future. The persistent interest in and mention of Helene's Jewish connection was to have damaging consequences.

Violent images of Jews were deeply embedded in the German psyche. Pamphlets appeared, depicting struggles between blond Aryan heroes and dark ape-men of the lower races, like the Jews. In 1919, Adolf Hitler made his first public appearance in a beer cellar in Munich, blaming the Jews for Germany's defeat in World War I. He stated, "We will carry on the struggle until the last Jew is removed from the German Reich."[14]

Jews were held responsible for the presence of syphilis in postwar Germany. In 1920, the infamous Protocols of Zion appeared, describing a secret plan by the "international Jewish conspiracy" for world domination. A popular German author, Theodor Fitsch, printed A Handbook of the Jewish Question, which compiled lists of Jewish intellectuals, writers, and musicians, as well as Jewish publications, which, he asserted, corrupted German culture. He gathered statistics on Jewish physicians and warned that they posed a menace to the health of German children.

As Helene grew, so did the Nazi movement. The first rally, which gave political voice to Nazi ideology, was held in Nuremberg, the imperial city of the Holy Roman Empire, in 1923. In 1924, Hitler was jailed for leading a failed putsch by 3,000 followers against the fledgling Weimar Republic. There he wrote Mein Kampf (My Struggle) while serving a prison sentence. He wrote: "The Aryan race is the bearer of human cultural development. It is in their nature—their blood—they are chosen to rule the world."[15] Mein Kampf was a vision of an apocalyptic conflict to come between Aryans and Jews.

There was the hope that Hitler's ominous visions and pronouncements would crumble under the weight and integrity of the democratic Weimar Republic. Lunatic fringe groups like the Nazis were far away from Offenbach, a peaceful town where citizens pursued their daily lives and small pleasures. Jews remained a mere 1 percent of the population of Germany. Intermarriage was increasing. By the 1920s one Jew in five had married a gentile. The Jews of Germany were the most thoroughly assimilated of all in Europe. To children of intermarried couples, like Helene, growing up in a nonreligious home, any accusations of being a lesser German seemed foolish, meaningless, and irrelevant.

There was no sense of doom for Offenbach Jews. During her childhood, Helene was a happy student, the champion in foil fencing, fresh, blooming, full of life, a wholesome portrait of German girlhood. Think of Dr. Mayer, a well-known figure in Offenbach, riding his bicycle around town, visiting his patients. He was appointed to a respected civil service position tending chronically ill patients. A music lover, he attended concerts, musical score in hand, whenever possible. Germany in the 1920s seemed a civilized and highly cultured country, and Hitler's rash suggestions transgressed the boundaries of reasonable minds.

Triumph awaited Helene in the immediate future. The Schillerschule (Schiller School) in Frankfurt welcomed her as the *horerer tochter,* the privileged daughter. In the 1920s, she received a quality education and brought fame to her school and the city of Offenbach.

*Dr. Bojunga, principal of Schillerschule, escorting Helene as
students celebrate her victory at the 1928 Olympic Games*

Chapter 5

THE SCHILLERSCHULE YEARS

Helene took the *strassenbahn* (streetcar) every school day from Offenbach to Frankfurt. The school was named for Friedrich Schiller, a German poet, historian, dramatist, and writer of popular plays extolling the ideas of liberty and human dignity, notions that swept through Europe in the 18th century. The school was a fitting place for Helene since her father was in complete agreement with Schiller's democratic leanings.

The school basked in the growing celebrity of its star student. Fencing replaced ballet as Helene's primary interest. Her day began with early-morning fencing lessons in the back garden of her home, followed by a rush to catch the streetcar, then a long school day, after which she had to complete homework assignments in the evening. Local fencing matches and tournaments at the Offenbach Fencing Club grew to include intense training for the German championship tournaments. It was a demanding schedule for the disciplined and energetic student who often arrived at school hungry. Somehow Helene was not served breakfast at home and would often scrounge food from school friends.

A younger schoolmate of Helene's recalled their days together at the Schillerschule:

For years and years we often talked on the streetcar. She transferred to my streetcar line from Offenbach. We had a lot of common interests and discussed our essay topics . . . the discussions of literary works, historical and political problems and the students' differing essay styles . . . My class teacher was Kladius Bojunga, also our school principal who was known as a philologist and as a brilliant German teacher. Both of us thought very highly of him and he always gave us something to talk about . . . Helene Mayer often probed me with questions about my viewpoint. . . .

I was always amazed at her great interest in school and our teacher's idiosyncrasies, because I saw her first as the world-famous fencer who every morning before school had to spend an hour fencing and who moved with great confidence in international circles. It seemed to me like a surprising trait of her personality that our little girls' problems with school were so important to her and that she treated me with so much liking and respect.

It gradually and probably much later became clear to me that she had an exceptional personality. What was striking was that her success in sports did not make her snooty or arrogant. When she occasionally, very rarely,

did tell us something about her other life that distinguished her from us, she talked about it in a very matter-
of-fact way. She was completing something that was given
to her and she had to fulfill . . . The fact that Helene was
half Jewish never played a role. It never came up.[1]

It is not known whether, as a child of 11, Helene wanted to distance herself from her Jewish heritage. However, in October 1921,
when Helene entered the Schillerschule, her father sent a terse
typewritten note to the principal, Dr. Bojunga, saying, *"Ich bitte
mein tochter Helene Mayer von der Teilnahme am Israelitischen
Religiousunter—richt zu befreien."* ("I ask you to excuse my daughter, Helene Mayer, from participation in Israelitischen religious
instruction.")[2] All schools required a designated religious affiliation
and offered religious instruction to their students. Clergymen of
different denominations visited school sites and provided lessons
to all those students who chose to receive them.

Dr. Mayer's decision to withdraw his daughter from religious
studies could not have occurred without thought and emotional conflict. He had a public and private connection to Judaism
although not in the religious sense, and he bristled at anti-
Semitism. His Jewish and German identities seemed compatible
and yet he chose to have his daughter excused from learning
about one aspect of her heritage.

To Helene, a busy youngster on the verge of adolescence,
growing up in a secular household with a Christian mother, religious instruction may have seemed pointless. Perhaps she
reflected the values of a new generation in a new era—making
her own choices, bent on assimilation and acceptance. Father
and daughter shared an enthusiasm for sports, fencing, and

education. In the area of Jewish identity, there were generational differences between them. Dr. Mayer, a liberal and respectful parent, seemed to leave this matter to his children. His request to excuse Helene from religious instruction deprived her of any public attachment to Judaism or any opportunity to talk and interact with a rabbi or Jewish educator. However, there is evidence that she had some slight contact with Jewish organizations; she took part in a sports meeting organized by a Jewish sports club, and gave a fencing demonstration in a Jewish retirement home.[3]

In these formative years Helene must have overheard talk at home at the dinner table, or among friends and family about the state of the Jews in Germany. Her father's affiliation as a member of Jewish organizations that fought anti-Semitism was beneficial and public. What was clear and important to Dr. Mayer, however, did not seem clear and important to Helene. To define oneself as a half-Jew was a tricky business. One had to make one's way through a thicket of latent and overt prejudice. The ties were tenuous; there were enough strong hints in Helene's environment that her Jewish half could cause difficulties.

Fencing was her consuming passion. Helene's victory in the 1928 Olympics swelled the pride of her fellow students. When the Golden "He" returned from Amsterdam, there was a note on the school bulletin board: "Our *Unterprimanerin* [12th grade student], Helene Mayer, has won the first prize in fencing at the Olympic Games in Amsterdam. Heil *He!*" One classmate recalled:

> I experienced her triumphant entrance into the school
> following her victory at the Olympic Games. On the
> school yard the smallest ones, dressed in light flowery

dresses, formed an honor guard and the principal, who was very German, greeted the half-Jewish woman in a formal address.[4]

A photograph showed a smiling Helene, smartly dressed in a tailored suit, her long hair topped by a flattering white beret set at a jaunty angle, carrying a bouquet of flowers. Dr. Bojunga, wearing immaculate formal wear, a long black frock coat and matching trousers, made the congratulatory speech. The girls lined the path as he and Helene made their way past this honor guard.

Newspaper and magazine reporters flocked to Offenbach and Frankfurt to interview the star. A delighted reporter enthused:

> There you can look into her room in her parents' house in Offenbach, adorned with the trophies, ribbons, garlands, diplomas, and even a photo of the Reich's president with his hand-written signature . . . The whole world loves her, as does everyone in this by no means small city. Strauss has given her permission to ride whichever horse she wants, whenever she desires. "I make frequent use of this permission," she answers my question. "Horseback riding is my favorite sport." She speaks without inhibitions as if we were old friends.[5]

Helene received an enormous number of congratulatory letters. Interior minister Carl Severing wrote:

> In recognition of the extraordinary achievements in the area of sports which you have demonstrated in particular

in the Olympic Games in Amsterdam, I award you the honor prize of the Reich's government—this badge, the highest honor by the Reich that is reserved for especially significant athletic achievements. The Reich's president will personally present you with this award on the occasion of a tea meeting on the 13th of October to personally express his respect for your successes.[6]

Many years later, Helene recalled another contact with President von Hindenburg. The president had written to Dr. Bojunga requesting that Helene be granted an additional leave of absence so she might make an exhibition tour of Germany. The principal granted the leave and framed the letter he had received from the president. When Helene returned to school, she was disappointed that she could not have the letter so she wrote to von Hindenburg. In return, he sent an autographed photograph that became one of her prized possessions.

Helene had an audacious streak, well aware of her ability to charm others, whatever their place in society. She fascinated the German public who had watched and applauded her rise to stardom. But some were puzzled and curious. In 1928, inquiries to Dr. Bojunga regarding Helene's religious and "racial" affiliation became more frequent. In one from Dresden, dated September 26, 1928, a professor wrote:

Dear Director,
If the newspapers are accurate, the Olympic winner Helene Mayer was a student in the 12th grade at your school . . . At our school we have lively and ongoing discussions about the claim that she is not of Christian faith.

I therefore take the liberty to ask you for a reply on the enclosed card. I ask you to regard my lines benevolently and remain yours faithfully and thankfully.[7]

Enclosed was a reply card with an empty space to fill in Helene's religious affiliation. Dr. Bojunga replied:

In response to your question I can tell you that Helene Mayer is of "israeli" faith. Maybe you can tell your curious students that the affiliation to this religious community says nothing about race affiliation, because one look at a picture of Helene Mayer shows every knowledgeable person where things stand. As is sometimes the case she mendels completely to the aryan side. What is most important to us is that she is a dutiful, open, and modest girl of true german character and true german spirit.

His letter closed, "With german greetings, yours, director."[8] In a similar response to another query, Dr. Bojunga wrote:

Dear Colleague,
Helene Mayer belongs to "the israeli" community in Offenbach. Her parents also belong to this community. The race affiliation is somewhat more complicated. She is half semite and half aryan. The correctness of Mendel's heredity laws have become particularly clear to me by looking at this family. Whereas the brother mendels completely to the semitic side, Helene mendels to the aryan side as you will probably already have noticed. . . . To the school, to me, and to other students, none of this matters. We appreciate

the girl for the modest, natural, and open child she is and whose personality shows only lovable traits.[9]

A word about Gregor Mendel, the Austrian plant geneticist who did pioneering work during the late 19th century in formulating rules of genetic inheritance. Before Mendel, the concept of blended inheritance predominated. It was assumed that offspring were typically similar to the parents because the essences of the parent were contained in the egg and sperm. These essences were "blended" at conception to form a new child. Mendel's work suggested the idea of "particulate inheritance."

His theory postulated that a gene passed from one generation to the next as a unit, without blending. Some genes had dominant or recessive characteristics that were reflected in a new offspring. Mendel's work aroused interest in the 20th century. In an attempt to "scientifically" explain Helene's "complicated racial affiliation," Dr. Bojunga relied on Mendel's work, going so far as to invent the verb "to mendel" to explain Helene's dominant, stronger "aryan features." Underlying his responses was an acceptance of a clash between Aryan and Semitic traits. Dr. Bojunga avoided labeling the Aryan side superior, but there was no denying that "aryan looking" was a highly desired, preferred status.

The director wanted to reassure his questioners that Helene was "a girl of true german character." As a nationalistic German educator, he knew what the physical characteristics of a good German were, just as he knew what "german greetings" were. In his mind, Helene could be both Jewish and German simultaneously. Her saving grace was that she "mendeled" completely to the Aryan side. What if she had resembled her older brother? Would she still be a good German? Would this make her "mixed racial status" difficult to defend? What was the position of some-one like Helene, with a Christian parent and a Jewish parent, who disavowed being Jewish and belied the assumed stereotyp-ic appearance of a Jew?

It was not only Dr. Bojunga who wrestled with these weighty issues. A prominent Jewish newspaper had quite another point of view. The paper printed a collection of quotes from other German newspapers of varying political views that took an interest in Helene's celebrity and her background. One piece, a poem in tribute to Helene, read:

> Suddenly the scene transforms
> a german girl, blond and admirable
> stands—three time winner—Helene
> the white glove at the foil,
> blue-eyed and in happy spirits,
> cheeks still red from the match,
> she who showed all European fencers
> the tip of her rapier.
>
> Female creature of modern times,
> she defeats plainly in her fencing costume,
> and behold, she's wearing blond braids!
> and ties around them a white band.
> A blue eye, a german skull,
> youth's grace in her countenance
> a well built girl from the Rhineland—
> and fences like the devil fences.[10]

A Jewish newspaper called the poem "an ironic contribution to race sciences." A sluggish and trite paean to Helene, it was replete with crude, easily recognizable stereotypes of glorious Aryan womanhood—"a german girl, blond and admirable . . . blue-eyed and in happy spirits . . . a german skull." In other words, Helene is a great fencer because she has the physical attributes of an Aryan. In a crescendo of delight, the final line "and fences like the devil fences" implies that patriotic fervor makes her fierce and victorious at all costs.

Another renowned Jewish newspaper in Berlin commented in an editorial:

> We are of the opinion that descent and religion have very little to do with athletic ability or inability. Helene Mayer competed at the Olympic Games in Amsterdam only for the victory of the German flag. But this superb example of this unbelievable "aryan racial doctrine" had to be mentioned here. For this blue-eyed and blond Helene Mayer is the daughter of our member from Offenbach, Dr. Mayer, which makes her a Jewish German.[11]

The Jewish press, representing an influential segment of the German Jewish community, responded with disbelief to the hypocrisy and preposterous claims of linking Aryan racial characteristics with superiority. In the eyes of the Jewish community, Helene Mayer was a perfect example of nonsensical racial ideology.

The notion of race as a determinant of the rise and fall of civilizations appeared in the writings of German philosophers and ethnologists in the 19th century. Purportedly scientific studies justified the notions of superior and inferior races, that racial mixing caused "decadent stock" and, therefore, less vigorous progeny. Scientific authorities on "racial biology" found ways to distinguish Jew from Aryan—the shapes of skull, forehead, lips, eyelids, a "typical Jewish posture"—were all studied. In 1926, a national competition was held to find the "best Nordic head," based on scientific measurements of skull size and shape. The words "Nordic," "Teutonic," and "Aryan" came to be used interchangeably to convey the idea of pure German stock. The word "Aryan" came to dominate the language of racial purity. The word "Semite" meant more than a descriptive noun meaning "Jew." It carried the stigma of inferiority and foreignness. The focus on Type A blood and Aryan physical characteristics ignored the crossbreeding that had gone on for centuries, producing a people who encompassed endless combinations of features and characteristics. The obsession with racial purity led to the establishment of 33 university-affiliated research institutes to study "racial hygiene"—the use of eye, hair color, and head shape and size to determine "aryanism."[12]

Hitler and his followers carefully added their poisonous ingredients to a stock of theories of racial purity and politically supported anti-Semitism. Helene was not aware of this dreadful stuff. She continued to enjoy her tasty and comforting *Linsensuppe*, lentil soup. It was nourishing, hearty, and thoroughly German.

In December 1924, Hitler was released from Landesburg prison and returned to Munich, the scene of the abortive 1923 putsch against the Weimar Republic. His five-year sentence for treason had been reduced to nine months. He emerged a hero, prophet, and undisputed leader of the Nazi Party.[13] In 1925, prohibitions against the party and Nazi newspapers were lifted. Bavaria, one of the states in the Weimar Republic, rescinded the ban against Hitler's speaking in public if he vowed to obey the law. A fervent public meeting was held in 1926, which enabled

Hitler's supporters to come together. It also tested the government's resolve to censure him. By 1928, enrollment in the Nazi party had reached 75,000; it rose to 100,000 a year later.

But in the national elections that year, Nazi candidates were seriously defeated. Some analysts declared the Nazi movement dead, hoping that Germany's gains in international status and improvements in domestic affairs would finish off the party. At the close of the decade many believed the precarious Weimar Republic would prevail. Cocksure of ultimate victory, Hitler assured his disciples that their duty was to arouse Germans to "fanatical nationalism" and lead them away from "the delirium of democracy."[14]

Helene's splendid career continued. She fenced in national bouts on German soil and in international events throughout Europe. She maintained her record as the German fencing champion through 1930. In that year she graduated with honors from the Schillerschule. A life-size portrait of her hung in the school entrance hall, commissioned in 1928 after her Olympic triumph. The painting was inspired by an overly romantic image of a knight, noble in bearing and aristocratic to the core.

Helene is painted holding her foil in her right hand, the foil gently touching the floor. Dressed in her immaculate, form-fitting uniform, her left hand rests on her hip, signature braids held in place by a white headband. She looks down, not out at the viewer. The painting is somber. Helene looks serious and contemplative. Did the artist see beyond the ebullient, confident fencer to the dark and melancholy events to come? The marvelous years at the Schillerschule were over.

Chapter 6

A LIFE INTERRUPTED: HITLER COMES TO POWER; HELENE COMES TO AMERICA

HELENE WAS POISED TO BEGIN HER UNIVERSITY CAREER, self-assured and confident of her future. In 1930, at age 20, she graduated with honors from the advanced program at the Schillerschule. She enrolled at the University of Frankfurt, in a city she knew well, to study law and modern languages.[1] Her eventual ambition was to join the German diplomatic corps, a plan that reflected her loyalty to Germany and her belief that she could serve her country well in the future.

During the first two years of university study, Helene spent 1½ semesters at Frankfurt and one semester at the Sorbonne in Paris. Her fencing career flourished. In 1930 the German Women's Foil Championship was hers for the sixth time. While studying at the university, she also fenced in national and international competitions all over Europe—England, Holland, Switzerland, Italy, Denmark, and Hungary.

In 1931, she won the European championship in Vienna.

The visits to European countries aroused her interest in foreign languages—English, French, and Italian. As a national celebrity, she saw herself as her nation's goodwill ambassador. Her fencing forays abroad made her more sophisticated and poised. She was referred to in a German newspaper article as the most famous member of the Offenbach Fencing Club. At the apex of fame, as an athlete and university student, Helene was far too busy to pay much attention to foreboding events in Germany.

Beginning in 1930, a severe worldwide economic depression alarmed the German populace. The government was overwhelmed and dealt ineptly with the crisis. The depression was exactly the kind of national distress the Nazis were waiting to exploit, giving them the opportunity to overthrow the Weimar Republic. The time was ripe for Nazis to take advantage of the fear and panic that gripped the country. In 1929, 1 million Germans were out of work. By 1930, the number had grown to 3 million; it would double to 6 million by 1933.

Paul von Hindenburg, the aging, revered elder statesman and hero of World War I, was lured out of retirement in 1925 to lead the country. He was the very model of the old-style leader—imposing, heavily mustachioed, bald—the stereotype of a typical German general. By 1930, the exhausted and perplexed president who regarded Hitler as an inexperienced, vulgar upstart had to come to terms with Hitler's increasing popularity. An election was scheduled for September 1930 to put in place a strong chancellor who would govern by emergency decree, if necessary.

Hitler campaigned. He gave a masterful performance, produced by Dr. Josef Goebbels, his brilliant minister for propaganda. Goebbels was 35 and extremely "un-Aryan" at 5 feet tall, 100 pounds, and walking with a limp. But he had an uncanny gift for public speaking and understood how to manipulate the emotions of a crowd. The Nazi propaganda arsenal included the use of posters, concerts, torch-lit marches, and impassioned orations. Speakers, selected from over 2,000 graduates of a Nazi orator school, fanned out across the country.

They accused the liberal politicians, Communists, Socialists, Allied powers, and particularly the Jews of treachery against Germany. A typical speech written by Goebbels exhorted listeners to:

> Throw the scum out! . . . Tear the marks off their mugs!
> . . . Take them by the scruff of the neck and kick them in
> their fat bellies on September 14th and sweep them out
> of the temple with trumpets and drums![2]

The tirades roused the public, and the Nazi Party received 6.4 million votes on September 14, 1930, making it the second most powerful political party in Germany. The Social Democrats still remained in control for the moment. Many Germans ignored Nazi gains; others applauded.

Until this time, there was no apparent discordance between Helene's goals and Germany's. The state had served her well; she wished to serve it in return. She represented Germany proudly. But this was all called into question with the stunning increase of votes for the Nazis in the September 1930 election. Deep fissures would widen into an abyss in the radically changing political landscape. Hitler's obsessive hatred of the Jews was spreading like wildfire, inflaming a susceptible public. Helene's exalted place in Germany was becoming jeopardized.

In April 1931, Helene suffered a tragic loss when her father died suddenly at age 55. A tender obituary in the Offenbach newspaper recalled his life:

Whoever saw him on Monday afternoon, like Offenbach was used to seeing him, the erect, still youthful, athletic person on his bicycle, riding from his work place to his private patients, and back from their sick beds to his pre-scription room at the compulsory medical insurance, did not want to believe it on Tuesday morning: Dr. Ludwig Mayer is no more. On Monday evening a heart attack put an early end to the happy, fulfilled working days of this brave man.

This is how Offenbach knew him since he settled here as a general practitioner almost 25 years ago. In 1922, the compulsory medical insurance employed him as their "Vertrauenarzt" (administrator)—a difficult job full of responsibilities, to which he devoted his full attention. He had to partly give up his private practice.

Not only the sick people, but also the healthy, strong and athletic people are mourning him. He was the president of the Reichsverband der Leibesübungen (Federal League for Sports.) He was on the boards of various sports clubs, rowing and fencing enjoyed his welfare, and he himself loved swimming (in spite of his 55 years, he was an outstanding diver) and whenever he found the time, skiing and ice-skating in the Alpine sun gave him back the strength he needed for his work. His love of sports has been passed on to his children.

But not only his athleticism—his other talent brought happiness to his work—his love of music. When Friday evening came, and with it the museum concert, Ludwig Mayer pulled out his pocket score and opened his soul to receive the great works. He came home from these concerts elevated and strengthened. They were the great celebrations in his life of work.

Does not all the strength that a living being has given remain with those to whom he has given it? Ludwig Mayer is dead. His memory may live in those who loved him, those whose companion he was, those he helped and those who honor him as a whole man and mensch.[3]

This heartfelt remembrance excluded any references either to his family or to his loyalty to the Jewish community. Because he was irreligious, his body was cremated rather than buried, as would have been the case in a traditional Jewish death. Dr. Mayer had escaped the onerous burdens that were being placed upon German Jews. With her father gone, Helene lost her last tenuous connection with Judaism.

Political events, fluid and unstable, continued on their dismal course in 1931. The economic situation worsened, banks collapsed, and Germany was drowning in unpaid reparation costs from World War I. President von Hindenburg agreed to meet with Hitler in an attempt to get him to support the conservative government's legal power. Von Hindenburg's strategy was to bring the Nazis under government control and avoid the total collapse of the state.

The president found Hitler to be an arrogant and loutish upstart, someone who had never held any public office; he felt it an affront that such an unseemly politician could have amassed so much public support. Privately, the president predicted that Hitler might become a future postmaster, but never chancellor, the key position in the government hierarchy. Other elite groups favored bringing Hitler into the government and approved of the Nazis rampant anti-Semitism. The Reichstag was paralyzed.

Warring factions in the parliament were unable to make the necessary compromises to block Hitler's maneuvers to achieve power. Hitler refused a deal to support the extension of the president's term without an election and presented himself as a staunch defender of the constitution.

Helene's educational pursuits were not impaired or interrupted by the unstable situation. She focused her thoughts on the upcoming Olympic Games to be held in August 1932 in Los Angeles. The Games would provide a welcome diversion from worrying affairs of state and the dire economic conditions in the world. Helene had great faith in her ability to triumph again. She hoped that a victory would revive the mood in Germany. Once again, she thought that success would help confirm her continued devotion to Germany. After completion of the Games, Helene's carefully conceived plan was to remain in Southern California for a two-year period as a graduate student at Scripps College in Claremont.

The German Fencing League was granted two spots for Germany's Olympic fencing team for the Games of 1932. Helene was chosen along with Erwin Casmir, who had won a silver medal in Amsterdam. At this time of economic crisis, the athletes themselves were called upon to raise 3,000 marks, a large sum, to cover the cost of their participation.[4] Helene was not only a superb athlete, she was also a superb fund-raiser. She went to Berlin and raised the necessary funds from enthusiastic sponsors who were sure that the one-time gold medalist would win again for Germany.

Los Angeles was a glittering, fascinating city, home to movie stars and celebrities. The city was well-suited to Helene's curious, adventurous spirit. It was an arduous destination for foreign athletes, who had boarded a ship across the Atlantic followed by car or train travel across the United States. But the setting was magnificent, the weather excellent, and despite hard economic times, the Games were well financed.

In 1931, the International Olympic Committee (I.O.C.) held a planning meeting in Berlin. The Weimar Republic was still in power although critically weakened by the depression and Hitler's ascent. President von Hindenburg met with the Committee. The I.O.C. awarded the 1936 Games to Germany, an important victory for this troubled country seeking opportunities to regain its international status.

The German planners visited Los Angeles in 1932 in anticipation of the 1936 Games. Dr. Carl Diem, a famous gymnast, sports historian, and educator, and Dr. Thomas Lewald, chairman of the German Olympic Committee, toured the Los

Angeles facilities. Pencils, rulers, and paper in hand, they took copious notes and measurements. The first Olympic Village, a 300-acre site 12 miles south of Los Angeles, included a hospital, library, and post office. This self-sufficient enclave had 550 bungalows to house the male and female athletes and staff. The auditorium held 10,000 spectators, and a magnificent Olympic swimming pool greatly expanded the facilities. Host countries were making substantial investments in the infrastructure surrounding the Games.

Helene, like all the other female athletes, was housed in a hotel in the city. An article headed "Queen of the Fencers" appeared in the *Los Angeles Register* at the time of the Games.

Her arrival at the Chapman Park Hotel created quite a furor among the other girl athletes, most of whom have short, bobbed hair and envied this pretty miss her novel coiffure—a physical counterpart as a Superwoman—her arm like iron, her grip like steel and her wrists as dainty as a ballet dancer's.

As the German teams were training for the Los Angeles Games, the country was paralyzed with a moribund central government unable to find solutions to worsening problems. Dramatic measures were necessary to deal with a restive and angry public and insoluble economic woes. In February 1932, a desperate President von Hindenburg agreed to run for office again despite his advanced age and fatigue. One week later, Hitler declared himself the Nazi Party candidate for president. The election was three weeks away. The Nazis held 300 mass meetings daily in cities and towns across Germany. They produced torrents of propaganda on film, leaflets, and on radio broadcasts. They received 11 million votes but still did not have a majority in the Reichstag.

A run-off election took place in April. The Nazis declared, "The basis of our struggle is hatred for everything that opposes us." Hitler used an airplane in his campaign, flying all over Germany to deliver vitriolic speeches that whipped the crowds into a frenzy of adulation and support. The crowds were swept up in a blend of invented mythic German history and Nazi dreams of redemption and superiority. The 1932 election was the last free election of the dying Weimar Republic.

In the run-off election, von Hindenburg managed to cling to the presidency. His cabinet, fearing Hitler's strength, banned all uniformed organizations of the Nazi Party including the storm troopers, a group formed in 1920 to be Hitler's bodyguards. Hitler was undaunted and continued to speak and rant, enticing his followers, favoring huge nighttime rallies that had a thrilling aura, terrifying and dramatic. He mesmerized the crowds as a prophet of glory coming to rescue a beleaguered nation. After hours of oration, Hitler often appeared dazed, dripping in sweat, pale and spent.

In June 1932, just two months before the Los Angeles Games, von Hindenburg appointed a perplexed newcomer, Franz von Papen, chancellor. Von Papen allowed storm troopers to resume their activities. The fading republic was no match for the relentless inspirational leader of an energetic, visionary party galvanized by furious devotion to their führer and his message.

What a relief for German athletes to escape this unsettled national domestic strife leaving squabbling politicians to figure it all out. Warm, sunny California beckoned. The athletes concentrated on doing their best, playing hard, and hopefully, bringing home medals. They looked forward to swimming in the Pacific, sunbathing on the beach, and attending a party or two in Hollywood, a welcome pause in a turbulent world.

Helene arrived in California with eager anticipation. She was in her prime, ready for her share of the dazzling extravaganza. Now 22, she was fit, poised, confident of victory and regarded as the finest female fencing stylist in the world. She longed for the chance to capture another gold medal. Instead, she took a disappointing fifth place. What the public did not know was that two hours before the final matches, Helene received the tragic news that her boyfriend, Dr. Alexander Gelhar, had drowned.[5] The entire crew of 60 men had perished when the German training ship, the *Niobe,* sank.

Before the Olympic Games, Helene had accepted a two-year stipend offered by the German Academic Exchange Service to study foreign languages at Scripps College in Southern California in preparation for a career in the German Foreign Service. An exclusive women's college in Claremont, California, 40 miles east of Los Angeles, the college had been established in 1926 and was one of the few institutions in the western United States to educate women for professional careers.

Ellen Browning Scripps, a newspaper publisher and philanthropist, founded the school, which became a well-known liberal arts college. When Helene enrolled, there were about 200 students. The campus was beautiful and tranquil, with tree-lined terraces, Mediterranean-styled buildings, and lush inner courtyards. The San Gabriel Mountains rose above the campus. Students on horseback meandered through brilliantly colored citrus orchards and untamed natural country.

Helene stepped into an embracing and refined new world, a protected place far from the world's woes and the confusion at home in Germany. The residence halls were furnished with original paintings by old masters, works by leading artisans, handwoven rugs, and antique furniture. Helene was in a Garden of Eden, a paradise on earth.

In the fall of 1932, Helene wrote in the *Scripture,* the student newspaper:

> My first visit to Scripps was during the Olympic Games with his Excellency Lewald, the head of the German Olympic Committee, and the German Student Exchange . . . In the aftermath of the Olympic Games I had time to imagine what the Scripps girls would be like. Would they resemble the type of "College Girls" [a much read German novel] . . . independent, uncontrolled creatures, or would they resemble the sweety, lip-sticked type of the moving pictures we saw in Germany? . . . Great and agreeable surprise to find them natural beings after all— nice, natural, interested . . . and this is a fact not a compliment! . . . What I noticed in particular was the friendly relationship between faculty and students. This was so new to me.

Friends recalled how she bowed deeply before each table in the dining hall at her first meal. "Charming, just charming," was the remark of a delighted student.[6] Helene came to Scripps with a celebrity's aura in spite of her unexpected defeat in the Games. She introduced a fencing program to Scripps. A Scripps publication on student life featured a photograph of her in her pristine white uniform, with an intriguing hint of muted sexuality, her mask nestled in her left arm, her right arm bent at the elbow as she gracefully raised her foil above her head. It described her:

> Miss Mayer's presence on the campus is a feature of the life at Scripps where each year there has been in residence one or more students from foreign lands bringing into the college life that note of distinction which always comes from cosmopolitan associations, whether in the classroom or in the field. She has persuaded the whole college to follow her own love of this sport, which is indeed as much art as sport.[7]

Helene plunged into her academic studies as well as fencing. She became president of the Franco-German club, the most popular club on campus, claiming 100 members. According to the *Scripture,* "The club has had several pleasant and informal gatherings around the punch bowl where linguists vied in recalling apt French phrases and German epithets."

The sun shone in California while darkness was descending in Germany. During Helene's first six months at Scripps, the Weimar Republic came to an end. In January 1933, 6 million Germans were unemployed. Public order was threatened; street fights broke out among Nazis, Communists, Socialists, and members of other political parties. The republic's death came in slow gasps as President von Hindenburg desperately tried to retain control. Finally, on January 28, 1933, the president named Adolf Hitler, age 44, as chancellor of Germany, a man who had never held any public office. The events preceding the announcement revealed a mistaken belief that von Hindenburg, as the president, would continue to pull the strings of the puppet, Hitler.

Hitler used the circumstance of a fire set by a Dutch arsonist in the Reichstag as a reason to propose an emergency decree that suspended fundamental liberties. Coupled with this decree was an Enabling Act that permitted the chancellor to promulgate domestic laws and foreign treaties without parliamentary approval or adhering to the constitution.[8] These decrees came to be the legal basis for Hitler's Third Reich. Germany's parliament, the Reichstag, was dissolved.

The cabinet, appointed by Hitler, approved a law merging the offices of chancellor and president. A new law transferred the power of both offices to Hitler. In 1933, the arrest of active political opponents put an end to open opposition. It became a crime to establish any rival political parties. Hitler's place was secure. His word would soon be law. The notion of the *Führerprinzip,* the führer principle, which stated that all laws, edicts, plans, everything concerning Germany emanated from Hitler, soon took hold. Hitler was the ultimate authority. The dictatorship was complete. All aspects of civic life—education, sports, professions, business, the armed forces, arts, and the press—were in Hitler's waiting grasp, to be dominated by Nazi ideology.

Helene's relationship with Germany changed abruptly with Hitler's victory. She was nestled in a cocoon far away, but this was only a temporary respite. Her long-term plans to return to Germany were in disarray. Her belief that she could continue to serve as a loyal German emissary, as an exchange student, was threatened. The fatherland was no longer her protector and benefactor. Scripps students gathered to hear a radio address by Hitler broadcast to the German public and the listening world. A fellow student, present there, recalled that Helene said "Verrückt, ganz verrückt!"—"Mad, completely mad!"[9]—to the savage deluge of Hitler's words justifying Germany's need for authoritarian rule and the destruction of its enemies.

After 1933, Jews were considered a danger to Germany's future. Hitler and his cohorts were ready with decrees and edicts to repress Jewish "infiltrators" who had influence over the press, trade unions, the Communist Party, and international capitalism. Worst of all, the Jews were carriers of "bad blood" and represented an enemy of unlimited resources and schemes for polluting the German nation.

With incredible speed, Hitler had laws enacted to stem the tide of Jewish "infiltration," robbing "true" Germans of their hard-won places. When Hitler came to power, there were thousands of published materials, 7,000 magazines and journals, and 4,700 daily and weekly newspapers, more than in any other European country.[10] That came to an end the moment detailed Propaganda Ministry guidelines appeared, delineating appropriate topics and styles for journalists, who then became rubber stamps for officially sanctioned views.

A cowed and obedient press paved the way for an avalanche of laws and edicts that tore away at the fabric of a civilized society. Within a few short months, the Nazis unleashed acts of terror and brutality. In April 1933, the first formal concentration camp was opened in Dachau, a Munich suburb.[11] The camp was large enough to hold 5,000 prisoners and "enemies of the state." In May, thousands of enthusiastic students and young supporters in celebration of the Third Reich burned 20,000 "undesirable" books in an enormous bonfire opposite the University of Berlin.[12]

Germans witnessed a carefully staged nationwide boycott of Jewish businesses. Storefronts were blocked by storm troopers who demeaned customers and made threats of violence to those who entered. The storm troopers carried signs stating "Germans: Defend yourselves—don't buy from Jews." In the same year, "non-Aryan" physicians were eliminated from their civil service positions in the National Health Service programs. Had Helene's father been alive, he would have lost his distinguished position in Offenbach as the health insurance administrator for the city.

In 1933, Mainz, that illustrious city that had claimed a long history of a vibrant Jewish presence and the place where Martin Mayer, Helene's paternal grandfather, had made extraordinary civil contributions, fell in step with Nazi ideology. The mayor instructed his registrar to inform him of every announcement of an upcoming marriage between a "person of German origin" and a "racial Jew." The information was to be transmitted to the regional Nazi Party, which would then "suggest" that the German partner reconsider the marriage. The regional officer had the duty to point out to the German partner the difficulties that might ensue from such a marriage regarding employment and offspring.[13]

That same year, citizens with disabilities were targeted for sterilization or death. Included were the mild to profoundly mentally retarded, those suffering from mental illness, blindness, deafness, and cerebral palsy. Many were put to death in hospitals, under orders from doctors.

In *No. 12 Kaiserhofstrasse—The Story of an Invisible Jew in Nazi Germany,* Valentin Senger, a Jew who grew up in

Frankfurt, wrote that his family's Jewish neighbors dismissed Hitler's appointment as chancellor.

> I give him six months. At the most. Not even . . .A flash in the pan. They were wrong. In May and June 1933, the bellowing storm trooper songs were heard on the streets. A hundred or more, dressed in snappy military uniforms and wearing caps with leather chin straps, sang a marching song, "When Jewish blood spurts from the knife, Oh, won't that be the day!"

Another song went:

> "Sharpen your long knives, sharpen your long knives, sharpen your long knives on the curbstone. Bury your long knives, bury your long knives in Jewish flesh. Blood has got to flow, blood has got to flow, and then we'll see. We say: Go fuck the freedom of the Jew democracy!"[14]

Raw outbursts of violent anti-Semitism escalated.

In Valentin Senger's school, a ruling was issued in May 1933 "prohibiting all greetings other than 'Heil Hitler.'" Some teachers resisted, producing sloppy, half-hearted salutes. The gym teacher wore a swastika pin in his buttonhole, and his students marched to the anthem of the Hitler Youth, "Unfurl our banner in the fresh morning breeze."

Some of Valentin's classmates had joined the Hitler Youth organization much before 1933. He listened to concocted faculty stories of Jewish physicians raping female patients, Jewish women acting as pimps, bringing orphan girls home to satisfy the lust of their husbands, and Jews who converted to Christianity but couldn't change their blood so they slipped into their "old ways" and left the church. "Once a jew, always a jew!" A biology teacher taught "racial science," and Valentin's mother helped fabricate a family tree to look as if they came from a Volga-German lineage. Skull measurements were taken and Valentin was pronounced "Aryan to the core!"

He lived at No. 12 Kaiserhofstrasse, next door to No. 11, home to the exclusive Hermannia Fencing Club. Helene was well-known on his street. Valentin recalled that "Every time she came home to Frankfurt, laden with fresh laurels, the whole street joined in giving her a festive reception. . . ."[15] After 1933, the Hermannia club moved away and the building was taken over by a Nazi "Strength through Joy" organization.

Did Helene hear of these things in Claremont, California? Were troubling incidents described in letters from home? If so, little mention was made of them publicly. Fellow students recalled that with the exception of her remark about "mad" Hitler, "she spoke rarely of politics . . . she was always very fond of Germany . . . she admired her country" and presented a cheerful demeanor. In March 1933, a Scripps foreign language professor, from the same department as Helene, wrote an article about conditions in Germany that was briefly quoted in *The Scripture*. "Some policies of the new government have already become apparent. Its anti-Semitism has been sorely felt by the Jews."

Helene did not see herself as an aggrieved Jew. To the contrary, she was a student freely pursuing academic inquiry and scholarship. A well-stocked library of uncensored and controversial books was at her beck and call. However distant, the book burning at the University of Berlin would seem to have been a catalyst for concern and dismay. And yet Helene did not even modestly protest this insult to free inquiry in her country.

Scripps College, like many other institutions of higher learning, was well-insulated. Problems of world affairs were not considered as important as national affairs. A great depression gripped the United States and reached its peak in 1933. Unmindful of events in Europe, Scripps students generously held benefits for local residents, collected food, and aided suffering neighbors. Occasionally, foreign news intruded. Mention was made in an October 1933 issue of the *Scripture* of a meeting between the school's trustees and German anti-Hitlerites, but nothing more. The frightening changes overseas took a back seat to the everyday hardships of life in America.

Helene carried on her bustling life at Scripps: studying French, teaching fencing, making friends, and enjoying her celebrity status. Social activities beckoned: barbecues at Bixby ranch (where Helene enjoyed feasting on "the husband of the cow"—her description of the barbecue), camping trips to the desert, a formal ball attended by the German consul in Los Angeles at what was then the largest private home in the city.

Helene was introduced to filmmakers in Hollywood; she gave technical advice for fencing scenes in films. On New Year's Eve 1934, she danced at a glamorous Hollywood party. She was vivacious, flippant, and flirtatious; men were attracted to her. There was an informal quality in her nature that Americans found unexpected and likable.

One student, who became her close friend, remembered meeting Helene for the first time at casual athletic events "where students interested in athletics met for friendly competition . . .

she always drew a crowd around her." She was lively, funny, always good-humored. She enjoyed misusing English words and inventing new words, combining bits of English and German. She rarely spoke of her family in Germany and seemed disinterested in politics, not unlike the other students. To close friends, Helene admitted to being half-Jewish; she said it was a burden and made her life difficult at times. But she didn't appear to be self-pitying, ill-tempered, or moody.

In March 1933, Helene experienced her first earthquake. At about 5:30 p.m., when many of the students were taking baths, the earthquake hit. As the young women jumped out of bathtubs and ran outside, Helene exclaimed, "There they are, naked as the dear God arranged them!"[16] Just a month later, an earthquake of another sort jarred Helene.

In April, just three months into the new regime in Germany, she was ousted in absentia from the Offenbach Fencing Club because of the new "racial laws." Nazi restrictions on Jewish athletes were enacted with alacrity and cooperation. Helene faced the insult of losing her membership, for reasons having nothing to do with her skill and fencing accomplishments, in a fencing club that she had made famous. But it was a decision she could not change.

In Germany, her family protested the ouster. "Hereupon they (the Mayers) were not suspended, but they were no longer registered as members,"[17] said a club spokesman, certainly a legalistic maneuver to deal with an awkward situation. This first public act against Helene, inspired by the Nazi regime and its ideology, was a stinging repudiation. It struck a vital part of Helene's being, her identity as a distinguished athlete.

There was no mention of the ouster in *The Scripture*. Helene herself kept the news quiet, perhaps hoping it was a capricious decision to be rescinded at a future time. To rock an unsteady boat on an unsafe sea could have unforeseen consequences. Better to ignore the ouster and think of calmer waters to come.

Helene was not alone. In April 1933, Jewish boxers and referees were forbidden from taking part in German championship matches. In August, the Jewish Macabbi Team was forbidden from participating in games held in Prague to unite Jewish athletes from many nations. In the same month, Jewish athletes were restricted from competing with Aryans in their own country. Sporting clubs were required to expel their Jewish members. Jews could no longer be lifeguards. Non-Aryans could not ride horses in competitions.

On August 1, Fritz Rosenfelder, a Jewish runner who belonged to a local sports club, committed suicide. The most virulent anti-Semitic newspaper of the time, *Der Stuermer,* praised the Nazis for Rosenfelder's death, stating, "We need no words here. Jews are Jews and there is no place for them in German sport. Germany is the fatherland of Germans and not Jews. Germans have the right to do what they wish in their own country."

A week later, in a town near Nuremberg, the city of spectacular Nazi rallies, Jews were banned from swimming in public pools. By the fall, Jews were allowed to train and compete only with other Jews. Many Jewish sports clubs closed, faced with unceasing hostility and the ubiquitous signs at sports facilities, *Juden Unerwünscht* (Jews Unwelcome.)[18]

In May 1933, the Minister of Education announced that Jews were excluded from "youth, welfare, and gymnastic organizations." Aryan youth were, at an early age, bonded to Nazi ideology partially through sports. They were introduced to *wehrsport* (military sports), whose curriculum included throwing wooden grenades and scaling walls as a means of body building.[19]

Dr. Daniel Prenn, who had represented Germany on the Davis Cup tennis team, was expelled as Jews were denied participation in international competitions. Jewish citizens and athletes who stayed in Germany faced dreadful isolation in their personal and professional lives. One outrage piled upon another, insult added to insult, each paving the way for bolder, more impudent measures to defy basic rules of civilized behavior.

To some journalists, sports figures, and democratic governments, there was a sense of foreboding. Yet there were no more than a few thousand Jewish athletes in Germany and while the anecdotal evidence was troubling, it did not seem to warrant serious censure. Anti-Semitism was a fact of life and tolerance toward it was worldwide. Although the Nazis were getting out of hand, it seemed best to ignore the situation.

In June 1933, Helene traveled to Chicago, where she won the U.S. fencing championship. She detoured briefly to Canada and re-entered the United States as a "permanent resident." When she returned to Scripps, another bombshell hit: She was informed that her exchange fellowship was rescinded based on "racial grounds."

The termination of Helene's sponsorship was a repugnant blow to internationally sponsored education, goodwill, and the earnest goals of Scripps College. The conspicuous withdrawal of her German-sponsored fellowship, like the ouster from her fencing club, was unrelated to her performance. It was difficult to believe that the withdrawal was accepted without question or protest. Perhaps college administrators of polite and decorous women's colleges, guided by current mores, chose to avoid becoming embroiled in controversy. In any case, the Scripps administration agreed to absorb the expenses necessary for Helene to complete her two years of study. It is likely that an anonymous donor paid her tuition and living costs.

The Franco-German Club sponsored a meeting about "Hitlerism." There were no specifics or elaboration about the contents of the meeting in the student press. Did Helene reveal that her German fellowship had been abruptly terminated? Were her fellow students informed? One aspect of human nature is to deny unsettling reality, especially as it escalates. The reaction to Helene's plight reflected natural impulses to maintain an orderly world in the face of unimagined transgressions. There was no outcry on the campus. One can only speculate about this lost opportunity for people to have expressed moral outrage against Nazi ideology.

True to form, Helene made the best of the uncertain state of affairs and she continued her studies. She read classics, Goethe, and the *Decameron* in the original Italian. In preparation for her Bachelor of Arts degree, she wrote her senior thesis in French, *L'influence du Symbolisme Français sur le Lyrisme Allemand (The Influence of French Symbolism on German Lyricism)*. Still devoted to Germany, she searched for connections with her country. In a printed excerpt in the *Scripture,* she described "the French inspiration for the spiritual tradition of Germany." She wrote of an influential French author who "comes before us [meaning Germans] as a prophet full of measure, beauty, dignity, and truth."

A terrible irony existed in Helene's admiration for justice yet blindness to grievous wrongdoing in Germany. Nor did the issue of anti-Semitism rouse the indignation of the small world Helene now inhabited. Anti-Semitic views were treated nonchalantly by many sectors of society, and were likely of little interest to most non-Jewish students at Scripps and elsewhere. To Helene, her Jewish connection was a nagging nuisance that she wished to put to rest.

In May 1934, before graduation, Helene, as president of the Franco-German Club, addressed the club for the last time. The *Scripture* reported, "Helene Mayer, the president, is giving us by way of a bon voyage present a disclosure of her life as Olympic champion." Helene talked about her fencing triumph at the 1928 Games, a retreat to a happier time, to memories of when she felt secure indeed and beloved as Germany's idol. That victory belonged to a bygone era.

Helene's attempt to relive the past seemed to be an avoidance of the disturbing reality in Germany. Inhibited by her intense patriotism and flight from her Jewish connection, she found herself caught up in a tangle of emotions: injured pride, anger, and worry about her future. At the same time, as a disciplined athlete she kept a stiff upper lip, presenting a persona self-possessed and in control.

Helene graduated from Scripps in late spring 1934. Her once-cherished goal of joining the German foreign service now seemed impossible. Knowing that her future in Germany would be uncertain, she had to figure out a strategy for surviving in the United States. Her assets were her degree from Scripps, her celebrity status, and her optimistic, self-reliant personality. At 24, she had to use her fame, ability, and wit to succeed. The two years at Scripps had been bittersweet to Helene, who—in spite of a warm welcome to the college and her bountiful good nature and adventurous spirit—experienced a sense of loss and estrangement in America. As yet unknown to her, she faced a confusing future in exile from her homeland.

California was an informal, welcoming place with a growing dynamism. Its climate, both political and cultural, was very different from her native country. If one had to be an exile in America, California was a good place to be. She was rescued by Dr. Aurelia Reinhardt, the president of Mills College, a women's liberal arts college in Oakland, California. Dr. Reinhardt offered Helene a job teaching German and coaching fencing. Although she longed for the day when she could go home to Germany, she drove her little roadster, "Asthma," up to northern California where she took up her new position in the fall of 1934.

Shortly after Helene left Scripps, an article appeared in the *Scripture*, reporting the experiences of a Scripps American exchange student who had been in Germany in 1933. The article stated that the student:

> . . . obtained many facts on the political questions which do not come to us through the newspapers and magazines. She was immediately struck by the great emotional pitch to which the Germans are keyed. They are ruled by their emotions rather than by their minds, and they feel that their need of a strong and forceful leader is very great. Hitler's followers believe that whatever he does is for the good of the country. Those who are not of his

party dare not express their feelings to other Germans, as there is no freedom of speech at all . . . The Jewish people are still insulted and cruelly treated and prohibited from holding any offices. One Jew when asked about the truth of the cruel treatment of his people said, 'As a Jew living in Germany today, I am lucky to be alive.'[20]

Scripps College was awakening to the menace of Hitler's Germany as Helene said her goodbye.

The consummate fencer arrives at Mills College in 1934

Chapter 7

MILLS COLLEGE

HELENE MADE THE 500-MILE TRIP NORTH FROM SCRIPPS, driving her "swanky" black roadster to Oakland for the 1934 fall semester. Like Scripps, Mills College offered open-handed hospitality to Helene. Mills, established in 1850, was one of the oldest colleges for women in the U.S. It was dedicated to studies in physical and life sciences, music, art, and foreign languages. Its scholars had pioneered in the fields of drama and child development.

Located on the Pacific Rim, Mills was one of the first colleges in America to offer courses in Chinese literature and Oriental studies. The 600 students came from 30 states and some dozen foreign countries. Faculty members were welcomed from various parts of the world.

"International understanding and tolerance are a part of daily living in such a democratic and scholarly atmosphere," touted a school bulletin. "Mills is the type of contemporary college founded in an era of agricultural development and rural spaciousness that makes in today's metropolitan area an educational oasis of 150 acres." The school offered "a life of quiet and contemplation, though it is located near a growing seaport and an industrial city," Oakland and San Francisco.

The bulletin continued,

The broad roads are convenient for automobiles, but campus gates discourage speed. . . . (One) has a sense of complete seclusion . . . treasures of earth and mind . . . bird song and falling water, leaf shadows and color of flowers fill the sense with grateful pleasure.

Many students excelled in sports. Helene could enjoy all her favorites, including tennis, swimming, and field games. She rode horseback on miles of bridle paths, and she was given the opportunity to develop a fencing program.

Helene arrived at Mills with her fame in tow. She was immediately conspicuous on the campus, although few were familiar with the details of her sojourn in the United States and the reasons for her unexpected exile from Germany. She was known as a world-famous fencer on a teaching fellowship in California. Indeed, Mills students felt lucky and privileged to have her on their campus.

Few could have foreseen that Helene would become the center of a controversy about U.S. participation in the 1936 Olympic Games, scheduled to be held in Berlin less than two years away.

At the time of Helene's arrival at Mills, the isolation and persecution of German Jewish athletes began to receive increasing attention. On September 25, 1934, as she was settling into her

Mills life, an article about Helene appeared in the *Mills College Weekly*, the student newspaper, that was headed, "Hitler Threat Detains Fencing Champion in US." It reported:

> Fraülein Helene Mayer, arresting, statuesque blonde, arrived at Mills College a few days ago, enthusiastic about the physical education department and anxious to begin teaching her class of twenty girls in fencing. The thing she likes about Mills, she says, is its tradition. . . . The German girl fears return to Germany because censors opened a letter to her mother allegedly criticizing Hitler. She cannot return to Germany in safety and, as she is here on a student's passport, she can stay in the U.S. only so long as she remains a student. A teaching fellowship awarded her by Mills College solves her immediate problem. . . . After watching this glowing girl of 23, Utenhoff of the L.A. Athletic Club remarked, "that girl can outfence any man on the coast and any woman in the U.S."

In this brief but provocative article, the reporter did not elicit any information about why Helene supposedly criticized Hitler or why she "cannot return to Germany in safety." There appeared to be little desire to probe or investigate the circumstances of Helene's exile. Dr. Aurelia Reinhardt, the president of Mills, who had been responsible for Helene's rescue, had to know more about her plight than was made clear in the article. The Scripps' administration must have informed Dr. Reinhardt of the circumstances surrounding the termination of Helene's fellowship at Scripps and her ouster from the Offenbach Fencing Club. The Nazi "racial laws" had left her stranded in a serious predicament.

Dr. Reinhardt had an opinion about everything from bobbed hair to the League of Nations. She was an imposing, vigorous grande dame who struck dramatic poses. She was committed to "international cooperation and understanding" and frequently lectured on her dedication to world peace. Her invitation to Helene served a socially responsible purpose and brought a magnetic, talented celebrity who would surely captivate the campus.

Helene was immediately accepted by students, who flocked to her fencing classes and to her class in beginning German. A glamorous addition to the campus, she had a flair for fashion—wearing scarves, capes, American Indian jewelry, white tennis dresses, sleek evening gowns, and her signature fencing costumes. Academic duties allowed time for training and travel to tournaments in the San Francisco Bay Area and other parts of America.

She was establishing herself as a captivating personality and an outstanding fencer on the American sporting scene. Like the students at Scripps, the Mills College students remembered her as "exuberant," "jolly," "fun-loving," and "unforgettable," a person who kept her personal affairs private but still developed a close camaraderie with students. Helene loved dancing, parties, and contact with men. One student recalled that Helene had singled her out for her favor; the student assumed it was because, like Helene, she was tall. Helene had a rule: She refused to dance with anyone who was shorter than she. Together, the two young women searched for taller dancing partners and attempted to monopolize the tall men for themselves. Another pal of Helene's recalled having her mother's car on campus. "A bunch of us girls and Helene piled into my mother's car and went to Luppo's pizzeria in North Beach [a questionable San Francisco neighborhood for girls from an exclusive college]. . . she was more fun than a barrel of monkeys . . . just gorgeous . . . I shiver with delight when I think of her!"[1] Helene's tall friend was also half-Jewish, providing an unspoken bond between them. As a contemporary of Mills students, Helene served as a role model for exciting, risk-taking behavior, which set her aside from older, more staid faculty members.

The jolly good times in California were in stark contrast to events in Germany. The emergence of the authoritarian regime gave rise not only to increasing restraints on the Jewish population but also abetted the ultra-nationalistic ambitions of the Nazi government. The year 1934 saw the strengthening of Hitler's wish to dominate the upcoming Olympic Games, to use them as a showcase for Germany. Albert Speer, Hitler's favorite architect, planned a stadium in Nuremberg, the city of the mesmerizing Nazi rallies. It was conceived to seat 400,000 spectators—a permanent home for the Olympic Games of the future, built to last for the 1,000-year Reich.[2] The stadium was envisioned as the center of a sporting universe destined to be ruled by Germany. (Only one building was completed, in 1934, a colonnaded reviewing stand for 250,000 spectators. The glow of its searchlights could be seen in Frankfurt, 130 miles away.)

In 1934, 1.5 million Nazis and ardent supporters of Hitler screamed, cheered, and stomped at the annual events of the Nuremberg rally. Hitler declared that he had chosen Nuremberg as the site of the rallies because the city reminded him "of the Olympic festival of ancient times." Blazing searchlights, loudspeakers, and torch-lit parades of thousands of marchers gripping the Nazi flag, with its black swastika, set the stage for the pageantry of the Games-to-come.

Tschammer und Osten, a dedicated Nazi and Hitler's sports minister, issued a decree in November, forbidding "any German athletic organization to affiliate with a non-Aryan. Anyone who sets himself up as a defender of Jewry no longer has any place in our associations. Every personal contact with Jews is to be avoided." This was a clear warning to non-Jewish athletes that they were to stay away from "the enemy" or risk endangering themselves.

As the winter of 1934 gave way to early spring 1935, Helene lived comfortably in her room in Mills Hall. She carried on with her teaching duties as she planned an active schedule to compete in U.S. fencing tournaments. In the early months of 1935, Helene and a select group of Mills friends attended a party in San Francisco aboard a German destroyer, the *Karlsruhe III,* which was on a worldwide training cruise.[3] Helene was acquainted with the chief executive officer.

At the party, Helene and her friends spent the evening dancing with the naval cadets. A student who was present recalled, "Helene looked spectacular in a black velvet gown. She disappeared for a week while the ship was in port—we hardly saw her." It was the student's assumption that Helene had remained behind for a sexual liaison with the officer. Although it was not yet a crime for a German citizen to consort or sleep with a non-Aryan, the liaison would certainly have been disapproved of back in Germany. Perhaps Helene and the officer never gave it a thought. Both were far away from home; they could do as they pleased. It was a time to live in the moment and hope for a future that would allow Helene to enjoy life in her homeland once again.

Soon after her madcap week, Helene won a West Coast fencing competition that qualified her for the men's open foil competition. This was the first time in the history of fencing in the United States that a woman had entered an open competition against men and only the second time in world fencing history. The *Mills College Weekly* reported, "The lack of women competitors has given Miss Mayer the opportunity of showing her outstanding ability against masculine competition."[4] Throughout her career Helene often defeated male opponents and took unrestrained delight in her successes.

In the open competition in 1935 where she took first place, an official at the event remarked, "Any mental hazard the men may have felt at lunging towards a woman soon disappeared when they met her skillful foil." Intensely focused, they engaged in a stylized courtship dance. Helene, with her robust sexual energy, was made for these encounters. Fencing was a reassuring affirmation of her determination and spirit, allowing her to set aside painful reminders of German rejection.

In May 1935, a reporter for the Mills paper had an exclusive interview with Helene. She described the walls of Helene's room "lined with gifts from all over the world and she counts among her choicest a beautifully inscribed book from Robinson Jeffers (a noted poet) and a humorous photograph of a pompadoured, black-bloomered fencer of the dashing nineties."

Helene had just returned to Mills after another victory as U.S. National Champion in the prestigious women's matches in New York. Helene mentioned that "should Germany invite her to participate in the 1936 Olympics, she would consider it an honor."

The Mills reporter continued and reviewed her fencing history:

After 1928, Helene admits that she had more fun fencing and traveling than she did in study and it was during these years that she did much to further the interest of German women in fencing . . . in 1932 she came to California to participate again in the Olympics. . . .

The reporter added Helene's conclusion that "by this time the Hitler regime had taken hold in Germany and women were forced to give up an idea of a professional life."

It would seem that Helene's musings about considering it "an honor" to fence for Germany in 1936 indicated her inability to come to terms with the crumbling connection to her country. She had been ousted from the Offenbach Fencing Club because she was half-Jewish and had lost her fellowship at Scripps for the same reason. Her statement about German professional women was untrue. It shed no light. For Aryan women, a professional life was possible for those who cared to pursue it.

The interview ended, "Despite her fondness for America, however, Helene admits a touch of homesickness and hopes soon to be able to pay a visit to her family in her homeland." Denying German reality, Helene expressed a longing to go home. When exile is involuntary, it must be a tormenting rupture that will not heal. Would a return to Germany give her an opportunity to prove her patriotism? Would participation in the Olympics restore her reputation, regardless of her Jewish father?

A report in a May 1935 issue of the *Mills College Weekly* entitled "Labor Camps for Women in Germany" offered an intriguing glimpse into the growing support by German students for the Third Reich. A German exchange student at Mills recounted a blissful summer experience, giving service to the fatherland:

Every girl that wants to receive a higher degree from a German university has to work for six months in such a labor camp. Every girl in Germany must give her strength for half a year to the fatherland. Germany hopes that every girl will make the sacrifice, although so far, the work is only compulsory for students. . . . In a German labor camp for women one finds daughters of farmers, workers, professionals, bankers. They all work with the same idea in mind. Help Germany. Now what is their work? They mainly help on farms. . . .

I will tell you about a day in such a camp. We were thirty girls. In a tiny village in Pommerania, in an old farm house we lived together. . . . The atmosphere, our bright blue smocks, and gay red bandannas made us forget who we were and where we came from. We stood all on the same step, on the same level. At 5 o'clock we got up, thirty minutes dancing, and then breakfast.

The morning meal was simple—a cup of soup and a piece of black bread. . . . Some went into the kitchen, others to the garden, others to do the washing. . . . The main group went to help the farmers. There they worked in the fields, did the sewing, looked after the children. . . . At four o'clock we were all back again and enjoyed our afternoon meal, consisting of a cup of rather thin coffee—called flower coffee because it was so thin you could see the flower pattern on the bottom of the cup—and two slices of bread.

After that meal, we sat together and sewed and sang; sometimes we danced folk dances and other times we prepared puppet plays for the children in the village. At 7 o'clock we assembled around the long horseshoe shaped table and to express our feeling of belonging we joined hands . . . with a feeling of satisfaction of having done something for the common good.[5]

These words conjured up an idealized, idyllic image of loving German girls, a vision of self-sacrificing, obedient young women, loyal to the state. Class differences evaporated as members of the German Volk gleefully united to help Germany. The Nazis were brilliant in attracting young people and exploiting their youthful zeal. If only a Mills student or school reporter had asked questions like, "What songs did you sing? What kind of lectures did the leader give? Would Helene Mayer have been welcome at the camp or in the village? Were there any Jewish students included?" Mills students were simply not given pertinent information to be able to evaluate the student's propagandist report.

This sanitized and synthetic account of the simple pleasures of serving the fatherland diverged sharply from a continued onslaught of punishing decrees against those outside the Volk. Many believed that each outrage would be the last. The Nazis, emboldened by passionate German support and by disinterest, disbelief, and confusion in the world outside, moved forward with their remorseless assaults.

Why did so few people speak out in that year? Ambivalent attitudes and animosity toward Jews were facts of life. Offensive Jewish stereotypes were accepted without question. Even in democratic countries such as the United States, the eradication of prejudice was a far-off goal. Prejudice dies hard. Commonly held anti-Jewish sentiments persisted in personal and professional practices. Unlike Germany, anti-Semitism never became a conspicuous, official instrument of governmental policy in democratic countries. But Hitler opened a Pandora's box of mixed feelings and uncertainties about endemic anti-Semitism in all western countries.

Dr. Reinhardt contacted the Emergency Committee in Aid of Displaced German Scholars and helped a number of them to find refuge and teaching opportunities at Mills. "Displacement" was not explained but was left vague and incomplete. It seemed as if the words "Jew" or "Jewish" could trigger an avalanche of jumbled feelings. The word "Jewish" was not mentioned in any article that appeared in the *Mills College Weekly* in 1935. The liberal college community, under the leadership of an activist president, provided an unparalleled setting in which to take a serious look at anti-Semitism gone mad. Mills College was unique in its special efforts to reach out to fleeing German-Jewish academics, yet there was a disinclination to face the awful events taking place in Germany.

Many believed there were gray areas between fact and exaggeration so that people were reluctant to think the worst. Millions of Americans, some on college campuses, felt that in light of the devastation of World War I, neutrality in foreign affairs was essential. The prevailing mood in Washington was clear—avoid becoming involved in the internal business of far-off countries such as Germany.

The preservation of peace was the ultimate goal, regardless of cost. Mills College simply echoed the debates going on across the U.S. A headline in the March 19, 1935, issue of the *Mills College Weekly* read, "100,000 Students to Strike in Gigantic Protest Against War." The question is raised on the editorial page, "Is Mills to Join the Strike?" and goes on to report that "a community forum debates U.S. neutrality policy—the best way to maintain peace is to 'keep out of foreign wars'—versus a stance of preparedness against oppressors."

There were prizes announced for "neutrality essays" from the Foreign Policy Association. As Americans debated the issues, increasing militarism and expanding offenses against Jews continued in Germany.

In January 1935, Germany regained the coal-rich Saarland from France. In March, Hitler announced the existence of the Luftwaffe (the air force) and proclaimed a military draft in defiance of the Versailles Treaty, which had imposed severe restrictions on Germany's military capacity. Thousands joined the Wehrmacht, a new term for the armed forces of the Third Reich. On a peaceful summer afternoon in 1935, rowdy Germans beat up Jews who had been frequenting cafés in the capital city of Berlin. Unexpected attacks could come anywhere at any time. Signs decrying Jews proliferated. Children were taught how to "spot Jews" and learned a new prayer: "Führer, my Führer, bequeathed to me by the Lord."

On September 15, 1935, the Nuremberg Laws, far-ranging measures against the Jews, were adopted and unanimously passed by the Reichstag. Their enactment was somewhat unexpected. The only law prepared for passage by the Reichstag that day had been a law forbidding Jews to display the Nazi flag, but Hitler had wanted to add something more spectacular so he proposed the Nuremberg Laws that had been under review by the Nazi elite for many months. By those laws, the state assumed the right to strip

Jews of their citizenship.[6] The laws also prohibited mixed marriages and made sexual intercourse between Jews and Germans a serious crime called *Rassenchande* (race defilement). Anyone with at least three Jewish grandparents was considered a full Jew, while people with two Jewish grandparents were considered *Mischling,* half-Jews of the first degree.[7] Even conversion to Christianity or any other religion could not save a Jew from his essential nature, a morally depraved *untermensch,* a subhuman. Jews had a new status as "subjects" or "nationals." Forced into a totally dependent situation, Jews were not allowed to call themselves Germans.

To be rooted, to feel connected is a profound human need. The new law was a breathtaking assault on Helene's essential sense of self. This unimagined social death, loss of citizenship, dealt a mental blow to the underpinnings of her persona. How difficult it must have been for Helene to reconcile her vision of herself and her "new" status. She had a triumphant past. She was the Golden He, the Teutonic-looking beauty, a national asset. Private feelings of disbelief and anguish had to somehow be repressed. And Helene managed to maintain a cheerful exterior in her daily life at Mills.

The Nazi government passed the Nuremberg Laws just 11 months before the 1936 Olympic Games. Outraged responses raised questions about America's commitment to participate in Games where the host country barred Jews. Two months after the laws were enacted, the *Mills College Weekly* devoted a lengthy editorial to the subject:

On November 26, 1935, the question was raised. "SHALL AMERICA PARTICIPATE IN THE OLYMPICS?" "The Olympic code which recognizes in the realm of sports the absolute equality of all races and faiths, is the direct antithesis of Nazi ideology," says Jeremiah T. Mahoney, President of the American Athletic Union. He has accused the Nazi government of discrimination on racial and religious bases against athletes who under the Olympic code are eligible for competition in the forthcoming Olympiad to be held in Berlin . . . .

The introduction of nationalistic beliefs, political and religious and national hatreds into an international sporting event constitutes a betrayal of sportsmanship and is contrary to the spirit of the Olympics. If the allegations are unfounded, the refusal by the U.S. to participate would be a grave injustice to the German government.

Quoted in the same article is the position of a Midwestern college:

It is not an American policy to dictate to other nations, that if the Nazi government decides that Jews, Protestants, and Catholics alike are taboo, it is Nazi Germany's own business and although we may think this attitude primitive and idiotic it will never become a government issue. But if Nazi Germany feels that her governmental decrees shall apply to other nations, America should not fail to withhold American teams in the 1936 Olympic Games. It is not yet too late to change the site of the Olympics to a country where real sportsmanship is assured.

The *Weekly* solicited its readers to respond. How about a response from Helene? What about her dilemma? Could she fence for Germany if she were no longer a citizen? Would she still consider it "an honor" to fence for Germany in light of the Nuremberg Laws? At Mills, Helene chose not to seek out a public forum to express her views. Perhaps her feelings were reined in by thoughts of her family remaining in Germany or perhaps she was carrying on a clandestine struggle to secure a place on the German fencing team.

Two weeks later on December 10, 1935, the following response was printed in the *Weekly*. It quieted the debate at Mills about U.S. participation in the Olympics. The response quoted from an official German publicity bulletin that put forth two opposing visions of the Games, one an "ode" to nationalism, the other to provide an arena for "international understanding and honorable struggle." The *Weekly* stated:

If the first, it was indicative of a definite, outspoken encouragement of that nationalism which characterizes the German political philosophy of the sacrifice of the individual and the group to the State. Then that much employed word of the present hour—"boycott"—should surely be extended to the question of our participation in the Games. If Germany is sincere in the promise of fair play to all peoples, including the Germans, then the U.S. should participate. As in any other international crisis our opinions are limited because we know not the validity of the information emanating from Germany. How much propaganda, pro and con, is as faked as a Hollywood stage set? Impartial investigation at this late date is an impossibility. Undoubtedly the U.S. will compete. The problem of the individual athlete who may be affected is too complex a human affair and involved too many conflicting sets of ethical values to be decided by the sway of public opinion.

Polite indignation was a more cautious approach than outright disapproval. Odious nationalism was somehow easier to accept than forthright acknowledgment of brutish behavior toward fellow human beings. In an effort to appear even-handed and practical, the response caved into some public sentiment. As the Games were fast approaching, the Mills onlookers, at least those writing for the newspaper, were loath to pursue a path that could lead to sentiment favoring American withdrawal from the Olympics.

Planning for the 1936 Olympic Games spanned a five-year period that had begun in 1931. The Games were awarded to Germany in the waning days of the Weimar Republic. Inexorably, the Olympic planners had to deal with the consequences of a staggering turn of events as the Nazis came to power and radically changed the composition of the Olympic Games. The American public, the press, and national and international Olympic committees were drawn into controversy unlike any other since the resumption of the modern Olympics in 1896. As the controversy grew, Helene, living her day-to-day life at Mills, found herself at the center of a gathering storm: Would the Olympic Games in Berlin lend credence to the Nazi regime? In light of the Nuremberg Laws, could Helene fence for Germany? Would she want to?

Chapter 8

THE OLYMPICS CONTROVERSY

INTENSE PUBLIC INTEREST AND DEBATE surrounded the planning for the 1936 Olympics. A lengthy, highly publicized process culminated in what was to become one of the most highly charged battles about politics and sports in the 20th century. Considering the latent and overt anti-Semitism, plus ignorance and disbelief in democratically governed countries about Nazi intentions, it was surprising that such a vigorous debate took place. Yet it was clear that some people had grudging admiration for authoritarian regimes such as Germany's.

During five years of planning, thousands of newspaper articles and editorials, rallies, radio addresses, debates, and negotiations reached a crescendo of discordant voices for and against holding the Games in Germany once the Third Reich had emerged. The process began in 1931 as a strenuous effort to bring Germany back into the fold of international sports competition. That year, the International Olympic Committee (I.O.C.) held a congress in Berlin. President von Hindenburg addressed the group and helped win support for Germany against Barcelona as the site of the 1936 Games.[1]

In 1932, Count Baillet LaTour, the Belgian president of the I.O.C. and an advocate of the Berlin site, announced that the plans had been finalized. The weakening Weimar Republic was awarded the honor of hosting the event. The Winter Games would take place in Bavaria's Garmisch-Partenkirchen and the Summer Games in Berlin. Dr. Thomas Lewald, a member of the I.O.C. since 1924 and president of the German Organizing Committee, with Dr. Carl Diem, a former athlete, sports historian, and founder of the German Sports University, were instrumental in petitioning for Germany's cause. They both had visited Los Angeles in 1932. Dr. Lewald had accompanied Helene to Scripps College. The Organizing Committee that became the German Olympic Committee chose a 250-acre site in Berlin.

Before Hitler had come to power in January 1933, he had already expressed his views about the Games. He derided the Olympic vision as "an invention of Jews and Freemasons, a ploy inspired by Judaism that cannot possibly be put on by a Reich ruled by National Socialists."[2] He was in complete agreement with Bruno Malitz, an avid Nazi spokesman and writer who declared in 1932 that only white athletes should be allowed to participate in the Games. Malitz wrote:

Frenchmen, Belgians, Polacks, and Jew-Niggers run on German track and swim in German pools . . . nobody can truthfully say that international relationships between Germany and its enemies have been bettered. There is no room in our German land for Jewish sportsleaders and their friends infested with the Talmud, for pacifists, political Catholics, pan-Europeans and the rest. They are worse than cholera and syphilis—much worse than famine, drought and poison gas. Do we want then to have the Olympics in Germany? Yes, we must have them! We think they are important for international reasons. There could be no better propaganda for Germany . . . no private clubs or associations will name the teams in the name of Germany and put Germany to shame. The State will name the team![3]

Malitz's words were prophetic. Hitler initially would have preferred a *Turnfest,* a gymnastics exhibition, rather than some messy celebration of games and team sports. Malitz identified key principles that guided the Nazi leader's racist doctrine and would supersede the Olympic Charter that pledged equality and fair play. It became clear that the State would control the Games.

Goebbels convinced Hitler that Malitz was correct in predicting that the Games would provide Germany with a world stage on which to trumpet the Third Reich's accomplishments. In October 1933, nine months after Hitler had assumed power, he summoned Lewald and Diem to a meeting. They were surprised and pleased that he gave tentative approval for the Games. After Hitler toured the site, his enthusiasm swelled. Twenty million Reichsmarks were initially allotted to the project.[4] Lewald and Diem continued as uneasy collaborators. Many believed that neither was sufficiently committed to Nazism. Even more, Lewald's father had been born a Jew although he converted to Christianity, and Diem's wife was also tainted by Jewish ancestors.

Preparations began in earnest. The Nazis moved with such

speed, determination, and bureaucratic skill to circumscribe Jewish participation that it wasn't long before disquieting information reached important people in the world of sport. It was said that German-Jewish athletes were being stripped of their rights to practice and compete. Alarmed at this, Count Baillet LaTour and Avery Brundage, head of the American Olympic Committee, met in June 1933 in Vienna to discuss the situation.

Three German members of the I.O.C. reassured the count that German-Jewish athletes would be permitted to try out for their national teams. This was the most significant issue. At the meeting, the I.O.C. insisted that Germany recognize their authority over the Games. Handling Hitler with kid gloves, LaTour told him to remember the Olympic inspiration—the Olympics were always held in ancient Greece, no matter what city they happened to be in![5] It was a too-gentle admonition to tamp down German nationalist fervor.

Just a month before the Vienna "assurances," Jewish community members in New York City mobilized and called for a boycott of the Games.[6] The boycott movement decried the Nazi ideology that:

> . . . regards chivalry, sportsmanship, and fair play as the vices of the weak rather than the virtues of the strong and which rejects Christianity for paganism and repudiates the principle of equality upon which both political democracy and sport are based, for the dogma of the superiority of the Aryans to all people."

In the same month, the Amateur Athletic Union (A.A.U.), the governing body of American amateur sports, began to investigate reports of Nazi bigotry. Under the leadership of Judge

Jeremiah Mahoney, the A.A.U. had considerable influence. It was their role to certify the American athletes to participate in the Games. It was agreed that the United States should not participate if the Nazis continued discrimination against Jews and Catholics. The A.A.U. assumed that the I.O.C. would ensure that the Games would be conducted "in strict accordance with the International Protocol." Fair play! No discrimination!

The American Olympic Association (A.O.A.), a planning group that later became the American Olympic Committee (A.O.C.), echoed the warnings of groups in opposition: If Germany did not give all athletes, regardless of race or religion, the opportunity to train for the games, "No American athlete would be certified." The planning group declared that since sport was the only true democracy in the world, the Germans had to enforce the basic concepts of sports and treat their Jewish athletes fairly. When the A.O.A. became transformed into the official A.O.C. under the leadership of Brundage, the once strong position of the group was immeasurably weakened as Brundage denied the gravity of the Nazi measures.

Brundage was concerned about the possible effectiveness of the boycott movement. He worked hard to counter their activity and became increasingly strident and critical as the movement grew. One of the three Americans on the I.O.C., General Charles Sherrill, reassured American Jews that German pledges could be trusted. The I.O.C. insisted on a written guarantee of fair play although there was ongoing news of widespread discrimination in Germany. Dr. Lewald was removed from his high office because of his Jewish ancestry. He was reinstated as "an advisor," only after intervention by LaTour.

Any promises from Dr. Lewald were suspect as he became a powerless mouthpiece for the German planners. In 1934, Bruno

Malitz, sports leader of the Berlin storm troopers, published *The Spirit of Sports in the Third Reich*. It was freely distributed to every sports organization in Germany and placed by the minister of enlightenment and propaganda on the list of Nazi preferred reading. Malitz reminded the German people that their sport was built on hatred. National Socialists "can see no positive value for our people in permitting dirty Jews and Negroes to travel through our country and compete in athletics with our best." Malitz reminded Germans that they had a special vision of athletic competition on German soil.

The American Jewish Committee sponsored a huge anti-Nazi rally in Madison Square Garden in New York City in 1934. Mayor Fiorello LaGuardia and other well-known dignitaries attended.[7] There was a spotlight focused on an empty chair reserved for the German ambassador, who had declined an invitation. The I.O.C., alarmed by the negative publicity, met in Athens to confront their German colleagues about the continuing reports of Jewish athletes being excluded from the Games.

The Germans reiterated their pledge "to admit German sportsmen of non-Aryan origin, provided they had the necessary capability." The I.O.C. accepted the statement as the pledge they had sought, but the Americans held back. It was decided that Brundage would make an inspection visit to Germany. Sigfrid Edstrom, a strong Brundage supporter and Swedish delegate to the I.O.C., wrote to Brundage:

> As regards the persecution of the Jews in Germany I am not at all in favor of said action, but I fully understand that an alteration had to take place. . . . A great part of the German nation was led by the Jews and not by the

Germans themselves . . . They are intelligent and unscrupulous . . . they must be kept within certain limits.[8]

In July 1934, Brundage traveled to Germany expressly to investigate the conditions of the Jewish athletes. He was not allowed to be alone with members of Jewish sports clubs and had to rely on an interpreter for information. He came away reassured that the Germans would abide by the Vienna promises and he believed that qualified German-Jewish athletes would be eligible to compete but also that few Jews were of Olympic caliber and therefore the fuss was a minor stir.

What was of supreme importance to him was that the Games be played as scheduled. The controversy continued. The *American Hebrew*, an influential New York Jewish newspaper thoroughly aroused by Nazi atrocities and the treatment of Jewish athletes, commented on Brundage's recommendation for participation:

Brundage led around by high henchmen of Hitlerism and in their presence received assurances from Jewish sports leaders that everything was pretty. Any American news correspondent in Germany could have "wised up" Mr. Brundage to the fact that the Jews had been intimidated and dare not tell the truth.

The paper used the term "Naziad" rather than "Olympiad" to convey its disgust with the indelible stamp of racist ideology on the Games. Emmanuel Celler, a New York Jewish congressman, was highly skeptical of Brundage's reassurances and instituted hearings in Washington to postpone America's participation. A month later, Brundage approved a 16-page pamphlet, *Fair Play for American Athletes,* that asked: Was an American athlete to be made "a martyr for a cause not his own?" It continued, "We the sporting public don't care about the Jew-Nazi altercation in Germany."[9]

The "Jew-Nazi altercation" was an internal German matter, to be settled in Germany. To Brundage, the question of participation by German-Jewish athletes in the Games was a matter to be settled in Germany and not in the international arena. A supporter wrote to Brundage, "Hitler has brought order out of chaos in Germany and is without doubt the world's greatest figure today . . . what this country needs was 12 Hitlers. Ha, ha."[10]

Germany, well-aware of the growing debate, acted to gain public endorsement. The minister of propaganda, in charge of domestic and international advertising, began printing a monthly newsletter sent to every sports center in Germany and abroad that was connected in any way to the Games. The newsletter was first published in five languages, then increased to 14. The newsletter ended up being sent to 25,000 recipients.

Each side worked assiduously to present its point of view. In the tense atmosphere of increasing polarization of opinion, Judge Mahoney became an unflagging foe of Brundage. Judge Mahoney wrote, "Germany is being ruled . . . by a class which obviously has no conception of the rule of natural humanity and friendship which governs sports."[11] Brundage accused Mahoney of self-serving behavior aimed at gaining Jewish votes for political ends.

Brundage's attitude against the boycott movement became more strident and anti-Semitic; he blamed New York newspapers, which, he said, were controlled by Jews, as the cause of the difficulties. Writing to his Swedish ally, Edstrom, he lamented:

> The Jews have been clever enough to realize the publicity value of sport and are bending every effort to involve

the American Olympic Committee. . . . Jews have communistic and socialistic antecedents . . . arousing class hatred in the United States . . . (we) must keep sports free from political, racial, or religious interference.

Despite the inflamed rhetoric, other A.O.C. and I.O.C. members remained conflicted and confused by the chasm between German promises of inclusion and their overt acts of exclusion. LaTour promised Brundage he would come to the U.S. to combat the Jewish boycott campaign, but he was furious that the Nazis had consistently violated their pledges of inclusion. Hitler had assured him personally that the charges against Germany were false. LaTour was on a seesaw of contradictory claims. In his role as chief diplomat for the Games, he tried to accommodate both sides. Lee Jahnke, who had served as assistant secretary of the navy under President Herbert Hoover, was an American member of the I.O.C. He finally lost patience with the endless hedging by the Nazis and asked LaTour to disavow Hitler. In January 1935 at a swearing-in ceremony in Germany for athletes who were to participate in the Games, not a single "non-Aryan" was present. Seven German-Jewish athletes, living in Germany, had each received a letter from their local sports authority, sent at the same time. The letter stated that their athletic prowess was inadequate so, therefore, they were eliminated from the Games competition. The Nazis had given themselves a convenient "out," a brazenly transparent lie. By denying proper training facilities and membership in credentialed sports clubs, Jewish athletes were unable to qualify.

The Nazis continued to avoid their pledges. Their distortion of the facts left boycotters like Judge Mahoney compelled to take further steps. In August 1935, a year before the Games, at the annual A.A.U. convention, Mahoney again urged U.S. withdrawal. He pointed to "irrefutable proof" of Nazi discrimination. After two years of negotiations, it was impossible for Jews to qualify for German teams. They were only eligible if they belonged to a Nazi athletic organization, but they were not permitted to join them. Mahoney noted that discrimination had widened to include Catholics, Protestants, and organized labor.

At this point, the U.S. press played an important role in calling attention to the Olympic issues. They wrote articles about the Olympic elites, the role of the athlete in national life, democratic versus totalitarian values, and the nature of sportsmanship—an endless tangle of questions and answers that defied resolution. Westbrook Pegler and Heywood Broun, well-known syndicated columnists, favored a boycott.

A Gallup poll in March 1935 showed that 43 percent of the American public favored one as well.[12] The debate grabbed the attention of a worldwide audience. Boycott movements arose in a number of democratic countries, including England, France, Belgium, Canada, and the Netherlands. By 1935, most U.S. newspapers continued to favor participation but raised many questions. The following is a smattering of views and headlines in the American Press on opinion about the Olympics:

In Nazi Germany, restaurants, foodshops, hairdressers display placards that Jews are not served—Call for the removal of the Games from Nazi Germany.

Dissolution of the Catholic sports organization in Baden. All members of the Berlin Police team who took part in a baseball match against the Jewish Sports Union were expelled from the Police Sports Union.

It is difficult to comprehend the stand of Avery Brundage, president of the American Olympic Committee who . . . remains obdurate in refusing to see that Berlin is not the right place for the Olympic Games of 1936.

Nothing contrary to the American conception of the "Olympic ideal"—Opponents are communistic and not interested in sports.

Economic pressure by certain organized minorities.

General Charles Sherrill, American member of the International Olympic Committee, warned that there is danger of increased anti-Semitism 'if Jews are scheming to get Americans to boycott the Berlin Games and keep 'me' [thousands of young Americans] from going there.'

"This is not an American conception of sport."

A systematic attack on Christians has followed the assault on Jews.

Jews do not get a fair break in Germany.

It may be too late to set the machinery in motion for transferring them (the Games) elsewhere.
Count Baillet LaTour, president of the International

Olympic Committee, said that after a half hour talk with Hitler, anti-Semitic signs would be removed.

Jewish War veterans of the United States start movement against US participation.

American Federation of Labor urges non-participation because of destruction of German trade unions.

Dr. T. Lewald denies that there will be any discrimination against Jews; says Games and German government are not connected.

National YMCA leaders urge participation.

Rabbi A.L. Feinberg urged end of agitation; says it hurts Jewish prestige.

15 Netherlands athletes, selected for competition, decline invitation.

Killing of Polish Jewish football player on field in Silesia causes many Poles to plan to avoid Olympics.

German Foreign Office denies reported death of Polish Jewish football player.

Rabbi Stephen Wise urges transfer to Vienna.

American National Society of Mural Painters will not exhibit as protest.

General Charles Sherrill amazed by criticism of his efforts—says no athletes have asked for boycott.

Canada to wait until England replies before deciding on participation.

Dr. Lewald Calls Mahoney Meddler—former Justice is Reproached for 'Offending against True Spirit of the Games.'[13]

Judge Mahoney made his last printed rebuke in October 1935 in a stinging, 12-part, fact-filled letter to Dr. Lewald. Despite Lewald's loss of status and influence in Germany, he continued to be a puppet spokesman, especially for American consumption. The judge's letter, a veritable "j'accuse," listed the ruthless escalating steps taken by the Nazis to thwart and demoralize German-Jewish athletes. He chastised Lewald for his humiliating role as a pathetic apologist for the Nazi regime. He wrote:

I recall that you were permitted to retain your position as titular head of the German Olympic Committee only through the intercession of the International Olympic Committee and the force of public opinion, and I fear that, lacking any real authority, you are being used as a screen to conceal your government's flagrant violations of the Olympic ideal of fair play for all, even the weakest.

In a withering indictment, recounted in precise details, Judge Mahoney exposed the terrorist acts of bias, citing specific reasons for American distrust. He ended on a symbolic note:

I believe that participation in the games under the swastika implies the tacit approval of all that the swastika symbolizes. . . . I believe that for Americans to participate in the Olympics in Germany means giving American moral and financial support to the Nazi regime which is opposed to all that Americans hold dearest. . . .[14]

With this denunciation, Mahoney brought to a close his long battle with the American and German Olympic elite. The *American Hebrew* published Judge Mahoney's entire letter.

Dr. Lewald had to respond, but he did not respond to the facts. Instead he called Judge Mahoney "a meddler," an intruder who offended against the "true spirit" of the Games. Lewald cited Brundage's support and that of other A.O.C. members.

The fact that these most competent gentlemen are entirely satisfied with our attitude and preparation, proves there is nothing in the German conception of the Olympic Games that might be contradictory to the American conception of the Olympic ideal.

On December 12, 1935, the *New York Times,* in a lengthy front-page article, reported:

The general convention of the A.A.U. of the U.S . . . closed . . . with a rejection of all attempts to keep American athletes out of the Olympic games in Germany.

The headlines read "A.A.U. Backs Team in Berlin Olympics; Rejects Boycott," "Mahoney Forces Lose Withdrawal Motion as Five Hour Debate Shows Defeat," "Inquiry is Voted Down,"

"Brundage New President—Mahoney Refuses to Run Again," and "Calls Result Moral Victory and Plans to Fight on."

The A.A.U., in a close vote, certified its athletes for the ensuing Games. Judge Mahoney resigned from the A.A.U. The enormous amount of publicity made it difficult for the A.O.C. to raise private funds for the Games and gave boycotters a platform from which to express their indignation.

For his efforts to insure the participation of German-Jewish athletes, Judge Mahoney was labeled an obstructing nuisance. As a result of Mahoney's resignation, Brundage now had two powerful positions: the newly elected president of the A.A.U. and head of the A.O.C.

The elderly founder of the modern Olympic Games, Pierre de Coubertin, was persuaded to support the Berlin site. In November 1935, Count LaTour also lent respectability by influencing Hitler to remove offending placards from public places in Germany.[15] Boycott activities were waning as the unstoppable journey to Berlin went forward although last-ditch efforts continued. A torchlight parade in New York City attracted 10,000 participants. In Paris, Philippe de Rothschild refused to take a French bobsled team to the Winter Games. A few scattered athletes bowed out.

There was a remarkable refusal by Dutch athletes to enter the Games. Weight lifters, wrestlers, and gymnasts did not attend. Individual athletes, track and field star Tollien Schurman, Wim Peters, champion triple jumper, and a Jewish boxer, Bennie Bril, turned away. Several artists and writers were against Dutch participation. They organized an exposition of their work in Amsterdam, infuriating the Germans. The exposition was called the D.O.O.D.—the acronym had a double meaning. It stood for

De Olympiade Onder Dictatu (The Olympics Under a Dictator) and *dood* meant "death" in Dutch.[16] In Austria, Ruth Langer, a Jewish champion swimmer, along with two other young Jewish women, Judith Deutsch and Lucie Goldner, rejected the Olympic opportunity. Anti-Semitism was strong in Austria, where the pools in which swimmers trained displayed signs that read "No entry for dogs and Jews." Heeding the recommendation of the World Federation of Jewish Sports Clubs, the three swimmers refused to take part. "We do not boycott Olympia, but Berlin," they said in a statement. The three women were immediately banned from Austrian swimming "due to severe damage of Austrian sports" and "gross disrespect for the Olympic spirit." The names of the Jewish swimmers were removed from the Austrian record books.[17]

Chapter 9

HELENE IN THE SPOTLIGHT

As THE GAMES APPROACHED, Olympic officials had to give at least lip service to fair play without prejudice. The A.O.C. and I.O.C. planners decided to insist that there be one qualified German-Jewish athlete. Bonded by supposedly cooperating Olympic Committees, Germany and the United States were united in a bizarre alliance to find and promote a suitable contender.

Once that was accomplished, the Games could proceed. The "award" went to Helene Mayer; the "designated Jew" on the German fencing team. Under the Nuremberg Laws, Helene was no longer a German citizen, yet she was invited to compete for her country. She would use this opportunity to suit her own agenda just as the Americans and Nazis would use her to suit theirs. The story of her inclusion in the 1936 Olympic Games is a sordid tale of connivance and deception.

In April 1934, eight months after she first came to Mills,

Helene traveled cross-country to New York City in quest of the U.S. fencing title. She won. The *New York Times* reported:

> With a ten-year record of repeated triumphs which brought her acknowledged pre-eminence in European fencing circles, Miss Helene Mayer of Offenbach, Germany, at present resident in the United States, arrived here yesterday. . . . Miss Mayer represented Germany in the 1928 Olympics and won the individual championship. In 1932 she again fenced on the Olympic team, but there is doubt as to what may happen in 1936.

> As a non-aryan under the present official definition in Germany, she has been expelled from the Offenbach Fencing Club of which she had been a member since she was 13. . . . Asked whether she would attempt to join the German team, she replied eagerly, "I shall certainly try. I have been assured that the pledge made in Vienna would be maintained and I would be given every opportunity"[1]

The door was opened. Helene had come to the attention of the American sports community as an outstanding athlete, the best female fencer in America, as evidenced by her New York victory. The press would closely observe her treatment as the worrying reports of Nazi persecutions persisted.

Although Helene desperately wanted to fence for Germany, to be tagged a "Jewish athlete" was a hard label for her to bear. The sticky, indelible stuff of Jewish identity clung to her. The irony was that Helene, who had no Jewish identification, became the standard bearer for German-Jewish athletes, a staggering burden but a potential opportunity.

For Helene, this role had a much hoped-for result. Despite the Jewish mantle she had to wear, she would again be on the world stage as a celebrated fencer. Despite her loss of citizenship, if she qualified she would fence as a German national and who knew what that might lead to. Her invitation to the Games took months of murky negotiations.

The press had a hard time sorting out German intentions as reports of deceptive statements and stonewalling persisted. Sportswriter Heywood Broun wrote in early 1935:

Decidedly we should not send a team to the 1936 Olympic games in Berlin. In my opinion, Avery Brundage, president of the American Olympic Committee sees the problem in too small a compass. Mr. Brundage says: "So far we have had no reports whatsoever, official or otherwise that Germany has failed to give Jewish athletes a fair opportunity to qualify for Olympic teams. . . . It is my understanding that in the case of Helene Mayer, champion woman fencer, German sports leaders have sought earnestly to have her return from the United States in time to represent Germany in the Olympics."

Mr. Broun continued:

Such earnest efforts must come from people lacking in addition to many other things, a sense of humor. It is a bitter irony to say to anyone in effect, "We hold you inferior, but that would not prevent us from using your superiority temporarily as an asset to the German team."[2]

The *American Hebrew* tracked Helene down in Canada in August 1935 and tried to clarify her position. In a cable to her, the paper posed four questions:

Did you receive and accept reported invitation to participate in the Olympics for Germany? Do you think in light
of continued discrimination, America and other countries
should withdraw? Do you regard yourself a refugee from
Germany? Did you know Nazi papers repeatedly and ten-
dentiously reported your suicide? Please reply collect.

Helene tersely replied:

Received telegram only yesterday. I cannot understand
newspaper write-ups because have not received invitation
from Germany to participate in Olympic Games. Unable to
answer your second question. Am absent from Germany
since 1932 and therefore do not consider myself a refugee.
Amused at suicide rumors. Helene Mayer.

She avoided direct answers. She parried with her questioners, and dealt skillfully and evasively with their queries, using fencer's maneuvers, now defensive, now offensive. Defensively, she feigned ignorance about the moral implications of Nazi bigotry.

An air of urgency and agitation dominated the grudging negotiations with Helene during the last months of 1935. Dr. Lewald arrived in the U.S. in September on a publicity campaign for the Summer Games. The *New York Times* reported that he planned to accompany a new zeppelin, especially built for the Games, on its maiden voyage to New Jersey in the spring.

He was quoted as saying, "The Olympics without America simply would not be the Olympics. It is unthinkable."

Dr. Lewald revealed that he was mailing a personal invitation to Helene Mayer to attend the German trials in February 1936,

> . . . with all expenses paid . . . We do not have any way of knowing if she has retained her skill after four years, but we hope she will come over. Believe me, we wish more than anybody in America that we had some Jewish athletes of Olympic caliber. But we have none, and I believe no one in America would want us to put a second-rate athlete on our team just because he is Jewish. That certainly isn't the Olympic spirit.[3]

Despite Dr. Lewald's announcement that he had sent Helene an invitation, she received nothing. In addition, there was no question as to the retention of her skills. She was fencing magnificently in the United States, and she remained of Olympic caliber.

On September 27, 1935, another long article appeared in the *Times* under the headline "Reich Recalls 2 Jews to Olympic Team—Invites Helene Mayer, a Fencer, and Greta Bergmann, High Jumper, to Be Members." The article said:

> The assurances were contained in a letter from Captain Tschammer und Osten . . . to General Charles H. Sherrill, American member of the International Olympic Com-mittee. [Gen. Sherrill had gone to Germany in 1935 to inquire about the status of Jewish athletes.] The letter contained Captain von Tschammer's official invitations, by letters, to the two Jewish women athletes. . . . The German Sportsleader

states he gives these letters "as evidence that Germany is acting entirely within the spirit of the Olympic statutes" and that "these members of the German team will receive the same treatment as other candidates, although they are Jewesses."

The article continued, ". . . the most convincing document is the letter addressed to Miss Mayer":

Dear Miss Mayer,
As president of the German Olympic Committee I have asked the chairman of the German Fencing Association to nominate to the Olympics the original ten. As you have been nominated already twice for the Olympic Games I am asking you whether you would take part in the Olympic Games in 1936 in Berlin.

If you agree, I beg you to consider yourself as a member of the pre-selected German team, which will definitely be composed in the Spring of 1936 after test matches. If you are prevented from taking part in these test matches, I am prepared to accept American sports tests as sufficient qualification.

[signed]
H. von Tschammer und Osten

The *Times* article continued:

The letter to General Sherrill comes as a climax to long consultations that he had with Reich leaders early this month. Asked tonight if he considered the letters sufficient assurance to warrant his speaking in America, General Sherrill replied that on the strength of them he intended to carry out his speaking program [to raise funds and support for the Games] and that part of it would be a reading of these letters.

On September 28, 1935, there was another communiqué from California:

> Special to the *New York Times* . . . Miss Helene Mayer, young teacher at Mills College, a fashionable school for girls in Oakland said tonight that she had received no invitation from Germany to take part in the Olympic Games and did not believe any had been extended or would be forthcoming. She declared that she believed some person or persons were using her name in this manner for the purpose . . . of adding complications to an already strained situation for some reason unknown to her. She would not say whether she would accept an invitation if it should come to her as a bona fide offer.

If Helene felt angry and manipulated, by whom? She did not dare name the powerful Sports Minister, Tschammer und Osten and his aides as the "persons" who were orchestrating the issuance of an official letter that had failed to reach her.

The invitation supposedly meant for her was sent to General Sherrill to win him over and bolster his search for support for the Games. Tschammer und Osten stalled as long as he could from offering a "bona fide" place to Helene perhaps in the hope that she would tire and disappear. As time ran out, ambiguities and questions about Helene's participation remained unanswered.

In an October interview with John Lardner of the *San Francisco Chronicle,* General Sherrill described his frantic attempt to settle the question of Helene's participation. Just back from Europe, he explained:

> I went to Germany for the purpose of getting at least one Jew on the German Olympic team and I feel that my job is finished. As far as obstacles placed in the way of Jewish athletes or any others in trying to reach Olympic ability, I would have no more business in discussing that in Germany than if the Germans attempted to discuss the Negro situation in the south or the treatment of the Japanese in California.

"Are you satisfied that Germany won't interfere with Jewish athletes?" Lardner asked. "Listen," replied General Sherrill firmly, "it may surprise you. I have spent the last few months getting a Jewish girl on the German Olympic Fencing team. Her name is Helen [sic] Mayer from California and I have succeeded. The Germans will put her on their team. That doesn't look like racial interference."

> I don't want to be sensational . . . but if we keep our team away from Germany we run the risk of starting the greatest wave of anti-Jewish feeling in history. Absolutely. In this country, right under our noses . . . There are about 5,000,000 Jews in America and about 125,000,000 Gentiles. If our Jews force us to stay out of the Olympic Games they will be taking a great chance with their own comfort and liberty. Feeling towards Jews has changed in

this country in recent years. I think it is a mistake on the part of Jewish leaders to stir up antagonism.

The general's advice was, indeed, sensational and frightening. He emphasized the view that American Jews would seriously endanger their fragile standing in the United States if they continued "to stir up antagonisms" against the Games. His admonitions had a sinister ring, echoing deeply held anti-Semitic beliefs about Jews as a bothersome, irritating people, fomenting unsettling controversy.

Although General Sherrill was convinced "the Jewish girl" (whose name he couldn't even spell) would fence on the German team, Helene still had not received an invitation. At the end of October, Judge Mahoney sent a stinging summary of accusations to Dr. Lewald in Berlin. His letter said:

You state that Germany has no Jewish material of Olympic caliber. Is it not because the outstanding German Jewish athletes are either dead, exiled or barred from training and from competition with Aryans, and that they are enveloped by a hatred so intense that it is impossible for them to develop and display their prowess?

It is not important whether or not Miss Helene Mayer is part of the German team. It is important that Miss Mayer has not been invited to participate in the German Olympic tryouts because of her non-aryan extraction until this month. It is important that it was four times announced that such an invitation had been extended to her, but as late as September 30, she had not received it.[4]

This was further damning evidence of the German Olympic Committee's efforts to customize the truth to suit their aims. The situation was heating up as the press exposed blatant misstatements. Dr. Lewald immediately issued a defensive reply to Judge Mahoney's accusation. "Helene Mayer, famous German–Jewish woman fencer, has accepted an invitation to compete for Germany in the 1936 Olympics in Berlin." To the newspapers he displayed the following cable from California signed only with the letter "H"—"Sickness delayed answering you and Tschammer. Acceptance left yesterday. Love."[5]

The sequence of events leading to the cable was obfuscated by lies and pointless statements by many spokesmen. "Assurances" of inclusion were fabricated for the press and propaganda. Were Lewald's pleas to Helene real? Were General Sherrill's assurances of Helene's inclusion in the Olympics credible? Did Helene actually receive Tschammer's letter? Did Germany really want her back?

Helene was so anxious to fence that she accepted the reluctant, if not coerced, invitation. She hadn't withdrawn as her opponents hoped she might. It was obvious that the invitation had been purposely delayed in an attempt to weaken and unnerve her, but she was tough. Up to this point, she had not publicly defined, nor had the Nazis, what was meant by a "bona fide" invitation. As a consummate disciplined athlete, she would endure whatever was necessary in order to compete as a member of the German Olympic fencing team.

If Helene prevailed at the Games, would it put the lie to the myth of Jewish inferiority? Would it confuse the German populace who were bombarded with the Nazi conviction of Aryans' unique physical superiority?

An editorial in the *American Hebrew* newspaper speculated about Helene's decision to accept:

> The real reason for Miss Mayer's acceptance . . . is probably that Messrs. Sherrill and Brundage and the other members of the American Olympic Committee put her on the spot by forcing the Nazi invitation; knowing very well what might happen to her family and friends in Germany in case she demurred.

> The stage has been definitely cleared for an Olympics showdown. Miss Mayer's appointment, under duress, in no way removes the Nazi ideology against those Protestants and Catholics who resent the liquidation of their sports organizations. . . . Helene Mayer . . . whose name has loomed large in these discussions, is reported to have accepted an invitation to participate in the Games. Just a week ago Miss Mayer denied that she had received such an invitation, thereby placing the Nazi government and American apologists in the position of liars. . . . A hurried invitation was sent. Since she had relatives in Germany, she had no alternative but to do as directed.

> There are those who will condemn Miss Helene Mayer for accepting the German Olympic Committee's invitation to compete for the Reich under the swastika. Her rejoinder . . . will offer the probability that she will win honors of the Fatherland and shame Hitler himself, with the admission that he is wronging the Jews of Germany.[6]

This paper viewed Helene as a helpless victim of Nazi and American manipulators, her position made worse by the climate of fear and intimidation in Germany. This was certainly a compassionate perspective from a Jewish point of view, but it was not Helene's. She was incapable of aligning herself with the Jewish community and the boycott movement. The inescapable "Jewish" label, the loss of citizenship, and the demeaning selection process propelled her to a bold course of action. She changed tactics. Her passive defensive stance was replaced by an unexpected offensive thrust.

On November 5, 1935, she demanded full German citizenship rights as a condition for her participation in the 1936 Games, as reported in the *New York Times*:

> Miss Mayer informed the German government and the Olympic Games Committees she would represent Germany only if granted full German citizenship rights, said a Mills College spokesman. "She has not received a reply to that offer. If the German committee and government refuse to grant such citizenship rights, Miss Mayer will decline."

This was an electrifying announcement, throwing the watching Olympic world into procedural disarray. Helene had acknowledged the reality of the Nuremberg Laws—German citizenship gone! She had decided to deal directly with the authorities, passing over the meddlesome media and interlopers. This was her battle; her character, her fencing skills, and her patriotism were at stake.

It took only three days for the German authorities to respond. On November 8, the *American Hebrew* reported,

... whereas German authorities asserted that Miss Mayer accepted without any conditions, officials at Mills College in Oakland, California where she teaches, said that she made it clear to the German government and the German Olympic Committee that she would agree to participate only if granted full citizenship rights.

The war of words continued. Helene took the chance that she could strike a bargain with the Germans. Privately, she asked the German consul general in San Francisco to use his diplomatic skills to fashion a negotiated settlement between her and the fatherland. The consul general was mindful that the Nuremburg Laws stipulated that a *Mischling* (someone of partial Jewish descent) had to have two Jewish grandparents and belong to the religious community. Helene fulfilled the first requirement, but not the second, hence her insistent disavowal on any link to Judaism—personal or communal. On November 18, 1935, Consul General Hinrich sent a report to the German Embassy in Washington, D.C.

According to the implementation regulations of the Nuremberg Laws, which are as of now only known through the American press, a number of non-aryans are granted the possibility to obtain Reichs-citizenship. Helene Mayer has two Jewish grandparents (on her father's side). She declares that she is free of any religion and that she has never been in touch with the synagogue community with the exception of her school years during which she had to participate in both Jewish and Christian instruction. She further explained to me that she feels all the more bitter about her present situation because she does not want to have anything to do with Jewish circles and that she regards herself in no way as Jewish nor does she want to be regarded as Jewish by others.

Regardless of the previously mentioned fact that Miss Mayer under no circumstances wants her petition with the Reich sports leader to be considered as a condition, she is now of the opinion that she can compete with conviction for Germany in the Olympics, only if she has certainty that she will be regarded as an equal member of the national community. She specifically pointed out that she has to live in an environment which would not understand, if she were to compete for a country which regarded her as a political underling.

From my last conversation with her I have gotten the distinct impression that she expects to be granted the Reichs citizenship and that—in the event that it will not be granted to her—she will have to take back her confirmation under the pressure of her current environment which she cannot leave right now. The pressure exerted on her by the press is particularly strong and she does not know how she will be able to escape this daily badgering any more.

Under these circumstances I would consider it suitable and advisable that the question about granting citizenship to Miss Mayer should be settled immediately and with a positive outcome. Otherwise it is to be expected that Miss Mayer who has an impulsive temperament and does not always weigh her words carefully will let herself be carried away into making remarks which will do us unnecessary harm considering the typical, prominent big spread of the American press.[7]

A look at the "diplomatese" in which the report was expressed shows a diplomat using his skills to make inoffensive recommendations to his superiors in Germany while, at the same time, presenting Helene's demand. Helene had to tread carefully, appearing to be respectful and loyal in presenting her case. One can assume that Helene had two goals in mind as the negotiations proceeded. Her long-term goal was to have her German citizenship restored. Her immediate goal was to be a member of the German Olympic team. She had to realize that she could not achieve both goals simultaneously.

Helene settled for the immediately obtainable one—a place on the fencing team. Perhaps a vague promise of citizenship would follow. Her request for citizenship was presented by the consul as a patriotic, magnanimous gesture to maintain Germany's reputation. Helene had the makings of a diplomat herself, fawning when necessary while maintaining an ability to stand for something that was of great importance to her. Fencing "über alles" was her prime motivation.

The German response indicated that the German Olympic Committee took the consul general's advice but only up to a point. The *New York Times* reported on November 26, 1935:

German Olympic authorities announced today that they had received Helene Mayer's acceptance of an invitation to compete for Germany in the 1936 Olympics at Berlin, and, at the same time, they assured the famous fencer she would be considered a full German citizen despite her Jewish blood. The problem . . . was settled by the decree of Nov. 15 whereby Jews were adjudged to be persons of 75 per cent, or more, Jewish blood. Miss Mayer does not come within this category, according to information here. . . .

[In San Francisco] Helene Mayer . . . said today she had received no direct word from the German Olympic officials regarding her competition in the games next year and that hence she would be unable to make any statement.

In a familiar stalling pattern, the Germans had yet again failed to inform Helene of the decision they had self-righteously proclaimed to the press. A determined Helene called upon the consul general again. Again he wrote to Washington, on November 30:

An Associated Press release has become known here according to which Helene Mayer's confirmation of her participation in the Olympics has not yet reached Berlin.

This morning Miss Mayer received a call from the anti-Olympic committee in New York who asked her to participate this coming Tuesday in a protest against the United States participation in the Olympics in Berlin and offered to pick her up in an airplane. Miss Mayer has declined the invitation with the explanation that the question about the United States participation in the Olympics is not a matter of an individual group but rather of the International Olympic Committee.[8]

By quoting the press release, the consul general reminded embassy staff that letters and assurances were coming and going but not reaching their intended recipient. He neither raised questions nor made overt suggestions, leaving that for his superiors, but he did caution that boycotters were making Helene's life intolerable. The dramatic offer of the boycotters to send an airplane for Helene was intended to align her sympathies with their movement. The consul general also made clear that Helene was a team player, that as an individual athlete, she felt she had no power to protest the decision of the I.O.C. that supported the Games.

The third and last report to the German embassy in Washington was sent on December 3, 1935:

> After Helene Mayer received a telegram from her mother yesterday, according to which her brothers are Reich citizens, and from which she concludes that Helene also has Reich citizenship, [Helene] has definitely decided to participate in the Olympic Games. She wants to go to Germany on December 21 of this year, or if the president of Mills College will not release her from her teaching position, in January.[9]

The problem appeared, finally, to have been solved. Her mother had declared her a citizen along with her brothers! Helene's mother, and, therefore, Helene, might conclude that she was one. It may have been a fanciful invention or perhaps Frau Mayer was deceived and purposely misled. Her declaration, manipulated or not, was a timely stroke of luck for German Games planners.

Did Helene now believe that she was a citizen and could return to Germany to train? There was no mention made of any documentation, written or verbal, that verified Frau Mayer's assertions. No German official denied or confirmed her statement. Her conclusion quelled the storm, for the moment, but the Nuremberg Laws were clear. They stated that a person with two Jewish grandparents was indeed "Jewish enough" to lose his or her citizenship. There was no escaping the fact that Helene had had two Jewish paternal grandparents and a Jewish father.

The Olympic Committees, Helene, the press, and the public were trapped in the Nazi regulations of defining "a Jew." Arnd Krüger, an eminent German sports historian of the Nazi era, explained how some commentators refashioned Helene's personal history. "Whereas American newspapers were only alluding to this, a Polish paper made much more explicit what they actually meant." He quoted the Polish source,

Helene Mayer was granted citizenship under the condition that she would disassociate from her father and denounce him and that she would sign a declaration that her aryan mother has conceived her from an extramarital aryan father.[10]

This theory was contradicted by another report, described by Krüger, that:

According to scientific Nazi examinations and measurements. Miss Mayer has only 25 percent Jewish blood in her veins.[11]

Supposedly these "scientific tests" took place in the United States. Despite these cruel lies, or perhaps because of them,

Helene won a spot on the German Olympic team. Ultimately, she was seen as a Jew by those Olympic officials who insisted that there be Jewish representation on the German Olympic team. To their great relief, Helene met the criterion. With the unofficial expectation that her citizenship would be restored, Helene finally fit into the Third Reich's game plan for the Berlin Olympics.

On one level, Helene acted with audacity. She had embarked on a critical crusade to rebuild her blemished reputation. Those who aided her cause, her family and friends and German colleagues, the unnamed Mills College spokesman, and powerful supporters of the Games, also chose to ignore the context of evildoing in Germany. All these players had an unwitting role in enhancing the Third Reich.

As 1935 drew to a close, the intensity of the Olympics controversy faded. The debate had consumed two years, with many issues—virtue, morality, and the place of politics in sports. Battle fatigue and the press of time quelled the boycott movement. Once Helene had decided to participate, opposing voices quieted. Thousands of athletes and countless spectators had lost their appetites for endless debates. Millions of dollars had been raised. The Germans were outdoing the Americans, constructing the most elaborate Olympic Village ever. Reports of Nazi transgressions were put aside in anticipation of better days.

During a tour of the Garmisch-Partenkirchen winter site LaTour noticed anti-Semitic posters lining the streets of the town. He insisted on speaking with Hitler, who responded that he would not modify "a question of the highest importance within Germany for a small point of Olympic protocol." After heated debate, the offensive posters were removed.[12]

The Winter Games were scheduled to begin on February 6, 1936. They took place in a friendly, unthreatening atmosphere that seemed a promise for the August Summer Games. A long, front-page report in the *New York Times* from Garmisch-Partenkirchen read:

No Signs of Racial or Political Prejudice Appear . . . As host to the Olympics, Germany is doing pretty close to a perfect job. Better organization and facilities for information could hardly be desired. Profiteering has been made impossible by the application of fixed prices and strict supervision.

Villages and arenas have been simply but picturesquely decorated with arches of evergreens and avenues of banners. In Germany's dealings with the public and the press courtesy and consideration are the prevailing notes.

 . . . it may be said on this eve of the opening of the Olympics that not the slightest evidence of religious, political or racial prejudice is outwardly visible here. Anti-Jewish signs have been removed from villages. *The Stuermer,* anti-Semitic newspaper, is being kept out of sight. A Jewish hockey player [Rudi Ball] has even been drafted for the German team. . . .

 . . . only sports count, and nobody thinks of anything else. . . . Every gathering place is filled with a chattering, polyglot crowd. The chatter is all of tomorrow, and the burden of it, in German, English, Polish and a dozen less frequently heard tongues, is "Let's go."[13]

Helene secured a leave of absence from Mills and sailed from New York on the evening of February 13, 1936, aboard the German liner, the *Bremen.* She had not seen her mother and her brothers, Ludwig and Eugen, for four years and was looking forward to a joyous family reunion in the lovely hill town of Königstein, near Frankfurt. On arrival in Germany, Helene told the press:

The Olympic Games were for international sportsmen and women and not for politicians. Everybody has been trying to manage my affairs. I've always intended going back. Once you've been in the games you will understand. It is a tremendous experience. And besides, I want a chance to win back that championship I lost in Los Angeles in 1932.[14]

Refreshed from her voyage and back on German soil, Helene gave another brief interview to an enterprising *New York Times* reporter:

She has informed local newspaper men that she received a personal invitation from the Reichs sports leader to return to Germany and compete for a place on the team. She accepted the invitation gladly and expressed surprise at "certain absurd reports" she read in the American press . . . [Miss Mayer's father] was a Christian of Jewish origin. Her mother is pure Aryan.[15]

This, of course, was nonsense. Her father took pride in his Jewish heritage and had not converted. Her remarks betrayed an uneasy posturing and altering of facts. Accustomed to being in the public eye and knowledgeable about the power of the press, Helene attempted to stop the erosion of her fading glory as a German sports diva. She felt compelled to substantiate the legitimacy of her invitation: it came from the boss, the sports minister. She did not mention her insistence on citizenship, however. The words "gladly accepted" glossed over the agonizing process she had endured in the U.S. What were the "absurd reports" in the American press?

Arriving from the United States, Helene hoped to return to her past life. A patchwork quilt of recollections—her family home, her father's bicycle, her mother's lentil soup, German beer, the Rhine, the rumbling of the streetcar on its journey to Frankfurt, the *salle d'arme* in the fencing club, the cheers of her admirers, the flattering newspaper articles, and the Golden "He" statuettes sold across the country were front and center in her memory. As an exile who left in 1932 for a two-year sojourn in California that turned into four years of enforced absence, she felt the sorrow of a life interrupted. She now hoped her banishment would come to an end.

Ironically, it was her Jewish roots, not her athleticism that brought her home. Because she was living in America, and highly visible as a former Olympic champion, she became the designated Jew, enabling the Germans to satisfy the demands for German-Jewish representation on their Olympic teams. But as the designated Jew she had certain flaws—no self-identification as a Jew, and no Jewish affiliations. Helene didn't take up the cause of her fellow German athletes who had committed the crime of being born Jewish. Their absence from the German team was not her problem. Helene Mayer was the window dressing appeasing those nations that were threatening to boycott the Berlin Olympics. She was not about to stir up trouble on the playing field.

When Helene left Germany for California in 1932, the country was still in the crumbling control of the Weimar Republic. Now, the fatherland was ruled by Hitler and a Nazi infrastructure that maintained coercive control over all aspects of life. On the surface, Helene saw commendable improvements—public order, clean streets, new buildings and roadways, a sense of national purpose, and enthusiastic preparations for the summer Olympics.

Even so, it was impossible to avoid the fact that fearsome, intimidating changes had also occurred. The friendly greeting of *"Guten Tag"* ("Good day") had been replaced by one arm raised stiffly in a "Heil Hitler" salute. Nazi police were everywhere and swastikas dominated public places. When she traveled to training facilities to prepare for the Games, there was likely the reminder of her ouster from the Offenbach club. When in Frankfurt, did she visit her beloved alma mater, the Schillerschule? Would she have seen her portrait still hanging prominently in the main hall?

Compulsory military service was reintroduced in 1935. On March 7, 1936, one month after the Winter Olympics and Helene's return to Germany, thousands of German soldiers, in defiance of the prevailing conditions of the Versailles Treaty, reoccupied the Rhineland. The action, however destabilizing it was to world peace, was greeted with misgivings but no direct response. Hitler's long-planned gamble paid off; the invasion did not threaten the Summer Olympics in any way.

In April 1936, a revised history book was introduced to German high school students. If she had flipped through its pages, she would have found a mythical history of the German people, an invented, delusional past "consciously excluding details." The study guide for the book stated:

> National Socialism demands history classes to be on the basis of race. This entails a new view of historical events. . . . The idea is to offer as much material to a history class as is necessary in order to understand the emerging of the German volk and the Third Reich.[16]

If Helene had visited her favorite bookstore, she would have seen a popular children's book, *The Poisonous Mushroom*. It was an illustrated account of the perfidies of the Jews, comparing them to poisonous mushrooms: they appear wholesome but are fatal.

In April 1936, as feverish preparations for the August Games were underway, another edict was announced: all "non-Aryan" children would be expelled from their public schools to be segregated into Jewish schools "to be established wherever 20 Jewish or half-Jewish children are found in a community. The child, either of whose parents is Jewish, will have to attend the Jewish school regardless of whether he has been baptized or not."

The minister of propaganda stated that "the presence of Jewish children disturbed the atmosphere." An inherent outcome of the Nuremberg Laws, this was another step toward the complete exclusion of Jews from German life. In this environment, it was folly to believe that somehow Helene would be declared a citizen or even an "honorary Aryan" as some had suggested. But there is no evidence that Helene sought out any official declaration or reassurance on the matter.

Helene trained in relative anonymity; Nazi-dominated newspapers hardly mentioned her presence. During her months in Germany, Helene lived amidst a protective and loving coterie of family, friends, admirers, and fellow athletes. Naturally optimistic, she drew on her resources as a committed athlete devoted to her sport. She plunged into fencing practice for the August Games, surrounded by well-wishers. Forget about politics, fair play, citizenship, and the press. Her best hope was to fence brilliantly, to become the forgotten Golden "He" again. Simply put, it was all about the contest. If she could win "gold" again, the magic moment of triumph might restore her honor.

*A deluge of Nazi and Olympic flags
at the 1936 Olympic Games in Berlin.*

Chapter 10

THE NAZI OLYMPIAD—1936

Germany saw the 1936 Games as a splendid opportunity to parade the Third Reich before a curious public and turn skeptics into admirers of the new state. Helene, too, was on a mission to put her best foot forward, to prove to her detractors that she was the finest female fencer in the world and a true member of the German nation. The 1936 Olympics was an unparalleled occasion for her, the culmination of an emotionally draining process full of deceit, moral ambiguity, and public disclosure of her Jewish antecedents. She needed to put all that behind her. She left the turmoil in the United States and nestled in the loving arms of her mother, who had pleaded her cause, and the fans who remembered her triumphs.

The encouraging embraces quelled any pressing doubts about her return. To dismiss a nightmare of defeat, she kept her eyes on the prize, focused on continuous training for the five months prior to the Games in August. The ability to endure suffering while showing a serene and confident face came from years of managing a celebrity status. Her worst dreams would be replaced by a new reality, a fencing victory in Berlin, Germany's urbane capital. She had once been the Golden "He." It must happen again.

It was not only ambition that moved her; she was also driven by a need to recapture her archetypal role as the radiant and beautiful Helene who would soften the iron hearts of her slanderers. Participation in the Games granted her a platform to prove her skill, allegiance, and staying power. The Nazis accepted the distasteful necessity of allowing this "half-Jew" to fence on the German team as a political necessity. It was as if the state and one individual had struck a toxic bargain, bereft of any intervening moral judgment.

Erwin Casmir, a premier German fencer and Helene's longtime friend and fencing colleague who was responsible for the line-up of the men's and women's fencing team, reported in an interview:

When we had committed ourselves to let all able German athletes participate in the Games, Helene's Mayer's ability was not even a question. I nevertheless had to inform myself about her present strength in fencing because we knew little about that and about the conditions for fencing in the United States . . . in order to participate in the training as well as in the qualifying contests. She qualified as the first participant and nothing stood in the way of participation after that.

I then reported the results to Reichssportführer von Tschammer und Osten who arranged the invitation by his excellency Lewald. At the reception in the Reichskanzle, the athletes were personally introduced to Hitler by von Tschammer und Osten. Hitler shook hands with Helene who was walking right in front of me, just like he did with the other athletes. There was almost no exchange of words during these introductions.[1]

Since she was barred from the Offenbach Club in 1933, Helene probably trained at various sites in Germany. The fact that she was back, and eminently qualified to fence, must have reassured many of her former admirers, eager to resume old friendships.

By the time Helene returned to her mother's home in Königstein, Nazi Party members were forbidden to have anything to do with Jews. If one was seen talking to a Jew in the street, the party member could face condemnation and punishment by a "Special Party Court." While people avoided speaking of current and future political events in Germany, everyone was talking about the upcoming Games in Berlin, the largest and most sophisticated German city with a population of four million residents.

Having lived in California for four years, Helene had much to learn about the elaborate planning for the Games. She recalled that Carl Diem and his excellency Thomas Lewald had painstakingly inspected the site of the 1932 Games in Los Angeles, in preparation for their showpiece in 1936. Helene knew both of them well.

She learned that Diem and Lewald, inspired by the drama of athletic competition, set out to startle the world with the sheer size, improvements, and innovations for the 1936 Olympics. A

The Olympic Stadium—Berlin, 1936

generous budget and boundless enthusiasm from Hitler gave them all the support they needed to bring their concepts to fruition. The lure of the Games in the hands of two passionately committed sports figures swelled Helene's desire to fence.

Alongside the talented planners devoted to athletics were the Nazi officials who exploited the event. Under Goebbel's ingenious tutelage, the Nazis had become proficient merchants of propaganda. They had learned well the political and emotional advantage of grand rallies, torch-lit parades, and blaring music, and the mesmerizing effect of huge flags emblazoned with black swastikas held on high. These techniques, perfected for the 1936 Olympics, would compel the world to take notice and applaud not only German athleticism but also the spectacular show. The Nazi Olympics would captivate the world.

A strong link to the ancient Greek Games was imperative to set the proper tone. The primacy of the human figure inspired the creation of the Olympic Exhibit aimed at a sophisticated segment of the German public.[2] The Exhibit traveled to major German cities in 1935 and 1936. It included plaster casts of superb Greek figures, athletes, and Greek gods, along with a history of the Games. The figures served as models that inspired German sculptors who fashioned large copies of the statues to adorn the Olympic stadium with suitably Aryan physiques.

The ordinary German citizen, one who lived in a more rural area, could visit the Olympic *Zug* or Olympic Caravan, a gigantic trailer that contained a series of huge exhibition rooms. The trailer contained models of the Olympic village and the new arena and sporting complex in Berlin. The first room in the Caravan, using the opportunity to pay tribute to the Third Reich, was dedicated to large photo murals of Hitler, surround-

*Torchbearer Fritz Schligen, middle-distance runner,
enters the Olympic stadium*

ed by Nazi flags, marching troops, and more intimate glimpses
of him in thoughtful discussions with his Olympic advisors.

Another innovation was the Olympic Bell. Designed by a
noted German sculptor, it was a dramatic symbol used "to
awaken" the German public to the coming events. The Bell was
almost 10 feet high. Its casting required 16½ tons of steel. Six
months before the summer Games, the Bell began its journey to
Berlin in a special vehicle donated by the German National

Railway.[3] The Bell was received in towns and cities along the route with receptions, civic ceremonies, and brass bands. Eagerly positioned Hitler Youth organizations awaited its arrival as it made its way to the capital. On the Bell's rim was the inscription, *"Ich rufe die Jugend der Welt"* ("I summon the youth of the world"), taken from a famous poem by the German poet Schiller. The "I" of the poem that had referred to Schiller became identified with Hitler, as if he was summoning "the youth of the world" to Berlin. He was imbuing himself with supreme authority, a pretender to the creative force behind the Games.

The boldest, most flamboyant addition to the unfolding production was the Journey of the Olympic Fire. Starting in Olympia, Greece, the site of the ancient Games, a relay of over 3,000 torch-bearing runners made their way across Eastern Europe to the German border. Hundreds of runners representing Greece, Bulgaria, Yugoslavia, Hungary, Austria, and Czechoslovakia passed the torch, one to the other, along the route from border to border. Impeccably timed, the final German runner was scheduled to arrive in Berlin on the opening day of the Games, August 1, 1936.

The multinational race had been conceived and supervised by Dr. Diem two years before the '36 games. An unextinguished flame, eternal symbol of the festival, was ignited by the sun's rays and passed on from runner to runner every half-mile of the 1,700-mile pilgrimage to Berlin. The run lasted 12 days and 11 nights. The beginning route to Athens was the most arduous, but weather conditions ranging from blistering heat to hailstorms in 5,000-foot passes did not delay the hundreds of runners nor extinguish the flame.

The route through Germany was saturated with members of Nazi party organizations. Onlookers listened to fanfares by

The flame is ignited—
the Olympic Games begin!

Hitler Youth trumpeters, church bells pealed, and town squares were illuminated by powerful floodlights. News of the nearly completed relay was broadcast by radio to Germany and the world. To thunderous applause, the ultimate German torch-bearer entered the outskirts of Berlin. Thousands of cheering spectators, 25,000 Nazi youth, and 40,000 storm troopers heard an earsplitting "Heil!" as the crowd lifted their arms in the Nazi salute. A sea of national flags, Olympic flags with inter-twining rings, and Nazi flags with stark swastikas filled the wide 10-mile-long boulevard aptly named the Via Triumphalis that led to the Reichssportsfeld. Here, 110,000 more welcomers awaited the arrival of Fritz Schligen, a sleek middle-distance runner.

Dressed in brief white shorts and a sleeveless vest adorned with a large black circle surrounding a swastika, he was flanked by six runners dressed in black. The runners glided down the Via Triumphalis alongside of him, maintaining their formation. They formed a perfect "V" resembling a huge bird, perhaps sym-bolic of the omnipresent stylized eagle clutching a swastika and Olympic rings. Greeted by almost hysterical crowds, Schligen entered the stadium alone, the final torchbearer.[4]

The Germans called sunny days "Hitler weather." On the first day of the Games it was overcast and cloudy, and rain threat-ened. But nothing could dampen the enthusiasm of the crowds, the thousands who had waited all night to enter the stadium and others who had attended the dancing, gymnastics, and sporting events of 100,000 school children throughout Berlin.

The 803-foot zeppelin *Hindenburg*, with swastika markings on its tailfins, hovered overhead, pulling an Olympic flag. En route to the stadium, Hitler with Olympic officials and other dignitaries cruised in four-door Mercedes convertibles along the Via Triumphalis. The 40,000 storm troopers kept the long boulevard clear of over a million cheering spectators.

In the late afternoon, Hitler, accompanied by Count LaTour and Dr. Lewald, entered the stadium. The three walked through a tunnel, making a dramatic entrance as they emerged onto the field. They were followed by the King of Bulgaria, princes from Italy, Greece, and Sweden, and the sons of Mussolini, the Italian dictator.[5]

Thomas Wolfe, a famous American novelist who was present at the Games, described Hitler's appearance:

At last he came—and something like a wind across a field of grass was shaken through the crowd and from afar the tide rolled up with him, and it was in the voice, the hope, the prayer of the land. The leader came by slowly in a shining car, a little dark man with a comic-opera mustache, erect and standing, moveless and unsmiling, with his hand upraised, palm outward, not in Nazi-wise salute, but straight up in a gesture of blessing such as the Buddha or Messiah use.

The Olympic Bell pealed as 4,000 athletes began their march into the stadium. A stately parade of 50 national teams advanced slowly around the track in alphabetical order. The Greek team led the way, honored for their country's founding of the Olympic Games.

To applause, the Austrians saluted smartly with the Nazi salute, the right arm stiffly extended forward, palm down. The French, attired in blue berets, raised their arms as they passed the reviewing stand. The parade continued. The British, nattily turned out in straw hats, decided on an "eyes right" gesture as they passed the reviewing stand, a disappointing move to the crowd. The American team, consisting of 383 members led by Avery Brundage, was unique in its decision not to dip its flag as it passed the tribune of honor. All the other flag bearers had dipped their flags as they toured the stadium. The United States flag was held high. When the Americans did their "eyes right," they placed their hats over their hearts.

One American sportswriter questioned the American team's refusal to give the Nazi salute in the opening ceremony. "When in Rome, do as the Romans do" was his admonition.

The last team to appear was the Germans, eight abreast, dressed in white, marching in perfect order directly behind the American team. "Deutschland über Alles" thrilled the spectators. The robotic "Heil Hitler" salute greeted the German athletes who stood at attention while the American team took their position on the field. In national solidarity, Helene stood with her peers, a standout figure and the tallest woman on the Olympic team. At 26, her photogenic good looks were undiminished, her figure full and striking, her gaze steady and assured. Some of the Germans present remembered her well. Younger spectators were unfamiliar with the Golden "He," particularly since the German newspapers had not publicized her return home. Journalists, who once wrote extensively about her fencing victories and charming "German" demeanor, were afraid to run afoul of the Nazi censors, who just might take exception to stories of her glorious past.

The opening ceremonies were drawing to a close. In the late afternoon the voice of Pierre de Coubertin, the aging visionary responsible for revival of the modern Games and who was unable to attend, was heard. His words were amplified over loudspeakers placed so all could hear both inside the stadium and on the streets. "The important thing at the Olympic Games is not to win but to take part, just as the most important thing about life is not to conquer, but to struggle well."[6]

In the reviewing stand, Hitler, clad in the drab brown uniform and black boots of a storm trooper, rose and said, "I announce as opened the Games of Berlin, celebrating the Eleventh Olympiad of the modern era." (He had been persuaded by LaTour to keep his statement short and simple. Hitler, accustomed to delivering four-hour tirades replied, "Count, I'll take the trouble to learn it by heart.") Pandemonium erupted after Hitler's proclamation. Hitler Youth released 20,000 doves into the sky. Trumpets blared. The German weightlifting champion dipped the German flag and recited the Olympic Oath.

We swear that we will take part in the Olympic Games in loyal competition, respecting the regulations which govern them in the true spirit of sportsmanship for the honor of our country and for the glory of sport.

The athletes raised their right hands in agreement. The "Hallelujah" chorus from Handel's *Messiah* completed the formal ceremonies.

As all this pageantry was underway, a small group in the United States made a last desperate effort to influence American athletes to disrupt the Games. It was a bold but doomed gesture of defiance against the Nazi Olympiad. Helen Stephens, a comely, 6-foot-tall Missouri farm girl and a promising contender on the United States track and field team, recalled:

A funny thing happened even before we pulled out of the dock in New York. I discovered two or three boxes of literature and letters in my cabin about the Jewish people wanting us to take a stand against competing against the Germans in the Olympics. They were wanting us to stage a protest of some type. I turned this material over to my coach, and I think she turned it over to the Olympic officials. That was the first, but more came later in Berlin—letters, telegrams—where people would write and tell you to get down on your mark and then refuse to run and say that you wanted prisoner so-and-so released from the concentration camps. I never could understand how those telegrams got through to Germany at that time. That was always amazing to me.[7]

Helene and her fencing class at Mills College

Chapter 11

HELENE AND THE GAMES

THE STREETS OF BERLIN WERE IMMACULATE, bedecked in flags and patrolled by storm troopers. Thomas Wolfe again illuminated the scene. "The whole town was a thrilling pageantry of royal banners, (the flags) flew fifty feet in height such as might have graced the battle tent of some great emperor."

The "gala city" was at its most hospitable. There was no price gouging, and food was plentiful. Berliners even consumed fewer eggs so that foreign guests were not deprived. Interpreters walked the streets answering questions from tourists. Jews who were not permitted by the Nuremburg Laws to fly the new German flag adorned their balconies and windows with the five-circle Olympic flag.

Opinions about atmosphere ranged from "a splendid achieve-ment by a new and energetic people" to a Berlin "odiously chau-vinistic and military." William L. Shirer, the great American journalist and historian of Hitler's rise to power, conceded that:

The Olympic Games held in Berlin in August 1936 afforded the Nazis a golden opportunity to impress the world with the achievements of the Third Reich, and they made the most of it. . . . The visitors, especially those from England and America, were greatly impressed by what they saw: apparently a happy, healthy, friendly people united under Hitler. . . .

And yet underneath the surface, hidden from the tourists during those splendid late-summer Olympic days in Berlin and indeed overlooked by most Germans or accepted by them with a startling passivity, there seemed to be—to a foreigner at least—a degrading transformation of German life.[1]

Official propaganda halted, muting anti-Semitic displays. The most vicious Nazi newspaper, *Der Stuermer,* was banned for the moment, but one "souvenir" issue managed to elude the authorities. The issue had on its cover an ugly-looking person labeled "Jew" jealously glaring at a "German" athlete. The ubiquitous slogan "the Jews are our misfortune" reminded the reader not to lose sight of the enemy within.

A political cartoon in the *San Francisco Chronicle* showed Hitler hanging a sign "We Stand for Racial Equality! No Discrimination!" Underneath the picture, the caption read, "Just during the Olympics!" Gloom was banished in Berlin. Civic leaders requested "a week of laughter" for the working people of the city. "The coming eight days will be days of jollity and cheerfulness. Prior to the strain of the Olympic week, Berliners should take stock of themselves, then with merry heart and friendly expression receive their Olympic guests."[2]

Herblock, the American political cartoonist, depicted a huge intimidating figure of a Nazi, muscular arms crossed, glowering at a perspiring, nervous Berliner, a good citizen trying to do his duty under the guard's watchful eyes. The beleaguered citizen is holding a declaration reading: "HITLER WANTS ALL GERMANS TO LAUGH AND BE GAY WHILE OLYMPIC VISITORS ARE IN THE COUNTRY." The citizen responds, "Ha ha! Look—I laugh so hard I'm crying!"

Parties and balls were held throughout the week. Hermann Göring, the most flamboyant member of Hitler's retinue and known as *der Eiserne* (the Ironman) who loved to dress in foppish, aristocratic outfits, staged elaborate parties in honor of the Games. Dr. Goebbels entertained lavishly.

Two thousand guests made merry at an estate that had been recently confiscated from a Jewish family. Goebbels wooed journalists. He saw to it that the 1,700 newsmen representing outlets from many nations were comfortably situated in a reserved area above the special box built for Hitler and his entourage. The first telex was used to send news of the Games and a zeppelin transported newsreel film from Germany. Film, radio, and photographic services were available for the first time. Although the screen was grainy, the Games could be seen in 25 specially equipped cinemas in Berlin.[3] The Nazis controlled every aspect of the Games—the planning, the pageantry, the press, the police, and the politics.

Francis Johnson was captain of the 14-man American basketball team (1936 was the first time basketball became an official Olympic event) that won a gold medal, defeating Canada. He provided, in *Tales of Gold,* a rare description of his impressions of Berlin in August 1936:

I met Hitler and Eva Braun one evening. We were in the Olympic Village just killing time, and lo and behold, here they came through the yard. They had come out to make a tour of the Village. . . . They asked us how we liked everything. Hitler looked just like you always expected him to look. He was just like you or me or anybody else standing there with his girlfriend. Eva was an attractive woman. . . . Actually, she was the only woman allowed in the Olympic Village. A couple of days before, a couple of German girls had tried to invade the compound and as a result had their heads sheared just like sheep.

Everybody in Germany evidenced the highest regard for Hitler, and anytime you'd meet anybody, instead of saying good morning, they'd greet you with "Heil Hitler" and a salute.

Whenever Hitler came to the stadium, there was tremendous secrecy. He had 10 big, black Mercedes seven-passenger touring cars, and you never knew which one he would be in. He'd be in a different one each day. They had a tunnel under the stadium, and all of these cars went into the tunnel, and from it Hitler could go right up into his box, which had a glass shield built around it. When he left the stadium, people packed both sides of the street just to watch him pass by.

One of the interesting things we found in downtown Berlin was that on every street corner there was a loudspeaker, and there was always music playing on those loudspeakers. But the German officials could cut in and broadcast throughout the whole city of Berlin anytime they wanted. In a matter of seconds they could shut down everything in the city through this speaker system. When an American won a gold medal, our national anthem was heard over these loudspeakers; it was quite a thrill to hear that.

The other unusual thing we saw was youth in training. They said it was the same as our Boy Scouts, but they had all of these youths out training, just going out and marching and popping their heels. It was actually a young military group. All of the younger people seemed to have everything, and the older people didn't seem to have much.[4]

The Reichssportfeld, a vast complex of arenas, practice fields, offices, parking areas, and the huge stadium built for 110,000 spectators, occupied hundreds of acres on Berlin's western border. Hitler ordered residents whose homes faced the complex to paint or clean their homes and decorate window boxes with flowers. The complex also included housing for the 328 female athletes at the Olympics. Closer to the city were other facilities and housing for the male athletes and staff. The brick and stucco buildings were a far cry from the bungalows built in Los Angeles in 1932. A brothel-like housing facility called the "Love Garden" was located in a woody area near the Olympic Village. It was available to the prettiest handpicked maidens to offer themselves to the German athletes. The maidens were usually sports instructors or members of Hitler's *Bund*

Deutscher Madchen (German Girls League). Babies born of these encounters would be cared for by the state.[5]

Helen Stephens, the outstanding runner from Fulton, Missouri, who dominated the competition and was dubbed the Fulton Flash, recalled the living conditions in Berlin:

> Our quarters over there were spartan. We had a dormitory that was a nice, new, modern building. We had a bed in there but not a real mattress. It was just a cotton- or kapok-filled thing. There was also a little stand and a light hanging from the ceiling. There was a community bath and showers. On the first floor we had a lounge that was nicely furnished to use if you had guests or if the press came. There wasn't any luxury connected with it. The dining room was nearby, and I remember they started out by feeding us green apples for breakfast and that heavy black bread that most of us had never eaten. So we raised a lot of Ned with them until we got some bacon and eggs and some American cereal in there. I think they were trying to weaken us.

> Those German girls who were attached to us as English-speaking guides could speak good English, and they were telling us that the German people were going to treat us nice while we were there, but that didn't mean that they necessarily liked us. They said they were going to beat the hell out of us come the next war, and in that very stadium there were tunnels underneath for air raid shelters. We weren't used to hearing all this. And all those training fields adjacent to the stadium were filled with thousands

of German schoolchildren marching around with broom-sticks and swords—the Hitler Youth, the Boy Scouts.[6]

A sense of critical urgency and bonding permeated Helene's reunion with her German teammates. Helene was back on familiar turf, one among German women who had qualified for Olympic competition. They were an athletic elite, allied in one vision of winning for Germany. In their shared quarters, all was *gemütlich,* warm and cozy. They spoke the language of the fatherland, ate the food of the fatherland, and gossiped together long past curfew about past triumphs and losses.

One can imagine an ebullient Helene regaling her colleagues with colorful "snapshots" of her life in California, humorous stories of fencing with gawky girls at Mills, known as "Helene's pigeons," and boasting a bit about her successes in the United States. Picture a poised, emboldened fencer, surrounded by an intimate group of "pals." Perhaps there was some unease within the group, a sense of bewilderment about her presence in Germany. Did the group allow the unpleasantness of Helene's Jewish status to rattle their good humor and camaraderie? Could they be loyal to Helene and to Germany at the same time? But this was not the time to talk of indecipherable events. Now it was time to buckle down and concentrate on the hoped-for victories.

Doris Runzheimer, a member of the track and field team, wrote: "We were together with "He" on a daily basis and were present at many of her fencing bouts, because she asked us to support her." In a tribute to Helene's past renown, Doris called her by her nickname, "He." Helene outshone the other two German female fencers, Hedwig Hass and Olga Oelkers. She fought for the gold against the Austrian fencer and 1932 win-

Helene demonstrates her astonishing lunge

ner, Ellen Preis, and Ilona Schacherer-Elek, fencing for Hungary, both of whom ironically were also "half-Jews."

> All reporters at the time remarked that each of the three had never appeared to be in better form. Their matches were fought in the amphitheater that was packed (as the fencing contests rarely were) and breathlessly quiet. The atmosphere was one in which the tension of competition was shot through with an undercurrent of race, politics, and personal destiny.[7]

Adrianne Blue, sports historian and author, also presented a gripping picture. The amphitheater where the Olympic foil competition took place was packed. They had all come to watch Helene Mayer who:

. . . some were surprised to see looked like any other *Fräulein,* with her flaxen hair braided and pulled around her head. Three of the greatest fencers of modern times were there—the reigning Olympic champion Ellen Preis, an Austrian; an ageing newcomer from Hungary, Ilona Schacherer-Elek, who was Jewish, and Mayer herself. All three had survived the elimination matches, and were among the eight women who were to face each other in the finals. The winner would be decided on overall points rather than on the outcome of any one match. Tension was high. The crowd was warned to be silent.

There was no sound as Mayer, who towered over Elek, lunged at her in the first of their encounters. Ilona Elek was small but quick, a left-hander. She had none of Mayer's classic style, and she had a shorter reach, but she was an excellent strategist. The crowd was willing her to lose. But Elek fought on. Playing to Mayer's weaknesses, she won their three bouts, 3 to 2, 4 to 4 and 5 to 4. But only time would tell who would eventually be Olympic champion.

Mayer fenced on, besting all her other opponents including every Aryan she faced. Mayer, it seemed, must be ahead on points.

Now came the most dramatic match of the Games. Mayer versus the reigning Olympic champion, the Austrian "Aryan" Preis. Mayer lunged; an agile Ellen Preis dodged. Preis lunged; big Helene Mayer eluded her with uncanny agility. Their match which evoked such rapt attention ended in a draw: 2 to 2, 3 to 3, 4 to 4.

Who would be the new champion? The officials added up the points all eight women in the finals had scored. Preis was, to the dismay of many, only the bronze medalist. Helene Mayer had to be satisfied with silver. Perhaps being an international *cause cèlèbre* had taken some toll.[8]

Richard Mandell also described the climactic Mayer–Preis match.

In an atmosphere so tense that the crowded spectators were almost too choked to express empathetic satisfaction or dismay, the two great athletes lunged stormily or dodged with uncanny agility. Almost miraculously, the scores for their three confrontations were 2:2, 3:3, and 4:4. A draw! However, points decided the placing of the victors. And there were no further matches of any pair of the three women. In the end Ilona Schacherer-Elek was the Olympic victor in Berlin.[9]

Many sports historians considered the Mayer-Preis duels "the most dramatic fencing match of the age."[10] Helene's buddy Doris Runzheimer was present at the decisive match and felt Helene was at a disadvantage. She wrote:

In 1936, the electronic score board had not yet been invented. Instead there were judges standing in each corner of the planche (a plank or platform.) During a match the judges decide who has scored or not. There were four international judges at the last crucial match with no German among them. It was a very suspenseful match, dubious judgments were made. 'He' unfortunately came in second.

The comment about the lack of German judges is puzzling. It was highly unlikely that a German side judge would be allowed to act as a partisan referee.

Close calls at athletic competitions where the stakes are very high are often discredited by disappointed fans. To Doris, a faithful member of the German Olympic team, the judges' decisions seemed deceptive and discriminatory. Others believed the judges had been accurate and fair. The coterie of supporters and curious onlookers in the *salle d'arme* realized that Helene was battling for more than a fencing victory. She yearned for her rebirth as an authentic German and a fencer par excellence. Such a victory might have obliterated the taunting Jewish label that so plagued her.

The outcome was a stunning disappointment. Helene had come so close to victory, only to be narrowly defeated by her Hungarian rival. Doris recalled, "She cried and said, 'It's not so bad that I came in second but I would have loved to get a little oak tree in 1936.'" Each gold medal winner received a little oak tree planted in a pot. Her plaintive longing for the "little oak," a revered icon in German culture and history, represented a rootedness in German soil and a deep identification with the nation. "'He' was given a lot of flowers for her silver medal. Because of the lack of vases, tubs were filled." A well-tended oak tree can live for hundreds of years. Flowers fade quickly.

John Woodruff, the first black American middle-distance runner who won a gold medal in the 800-meter event, accepted his oak tree with reverence and respect:

I was happy to win that race because that's what I went over to Germany to do. I've always had that feeling of winning. When I got down on the mark, the only thing that I ever had on my mind was to win the race. I never got into any race with the feeling that I wasn't going to win.

Each of us who won a gold medal in Germany received an oak tree. I brought mine home with me, but when I got home I was notified that the tree had to be shipped to Washington, D.C., to the Agriculture Department because they had to check it for any bugs that might be on it. Then it was shipped back to me, and when I got it, it was almost dead.

I turned it over to Dr. John Lewis, the botany teacher at my high school. He revived it and planted it on the lawn of the Carnegie Library there in Connellsville [Ohio]. Then when the Connellsville Stadium was built, they moved the tree out to the stadium. There it stood for many years before anybody knew anything about it.

Then one weekend when I was back home I went to the local paper, the *Connellsville Courier,* and told them that it would be nice if somebody would put something out there by the tree so that the young kids would know what it represented. So they raised the money for a plaque, and now everybody knows the history of that tree.[11]

As Helene and the two other fencers awaited the victory celebration for the presentation of medals, dramatic performances by a diverse group of athletes stirred great interest. Many of these events challenged Nazi claims of Aryan superiority. A Korean won the marathon run; Japanese swimmers and divers performed well; the Egyptians excelled in weight lifting; Jesse Owens, a black sharecropper's son raised in Alabama, won four gold medals and set a world's record for the 100- and 400-meter dash. Two other black American athletes won gold and silver in the high jump. More strident Nazis sneeringly referred to them as "black auxiliaries," a refusal to acknowledge them as human beings. Hitler managed to avoid shaking hands with these champions.

Anti-Semitism had a shameful outcome when two Jewish-American runners, Marty Glickman and Sam Stoller, were excluded by American sports officials from the 400-meter relay team. It was not accidental that they were the only members of the American Olympic team who did not compete in any event in Berlin. Ironically, a Hungarian woman won the high jump with a leap of 1.6 meters, exactly the height Gretel Bergmann, the German-Jewish athlete, had attained when she was ousted and declared not to be of Olympic caliber.

From Europe, there were victories for Holland's champion swimmer, who won three gold medals. The French excelled in cycling, the Italians in fencing, the Swedes and Hungarians in wrestling. But the Germans had good reason to celebrate as well. They won the most medals—89 in all, which included 33 golds. The Americans dominated the track and field events but their medal tally, 56, was second for the first time since the modern Games began in 1896.

Leni Riefenstahl, the brilliant cinematographer and official documentarian, captured almost all the events—250 hours of film were shot, requiring 18 months of editing to produce a three-hour film.[12] *Olympia,* considered the foremost sports film ever made, glorified the Nazi regime and the assembled athletes.

Notable Germans in Berlin celebrated with another spree of wild parties. Helene, who loved a good time and the attention of men, had not reclaimed her celebrity status and was not invited to those festivities. Helen Stephens won the 100-meter race, in an astonishing time, 11.5 seconds, and anchored the 400-meter relay. Her blonde good looks and decisive victory caught the attention of the Nazi luminaries. She was the only American athlete invited to meet Hitler at the 1936 Games.

They ushered us into a glass-enclosed room behind Hitler's box in the stadium. In a few minutes the doors opened, and about 15 black-shirted guards came in, lined up, and stood at attention. They had those big German Lugers on their belts, and they unsnapped them. Why, it looked like an assassination squad! Then Hitler came in with his interpreter. He gave me a little Nazi salute, and I thought, "I'm not going to salute you." So I extended my hand and gave him a good ol' Missouri handshake.

Well, immediately Hitler goes for the jugular vein. He gets ahold of my fanny, and he begins to squeeze and pinch and hug me up, and he said, "You're a true Aryan type. You should be running for Germany." So after he gave me the once-over and a full massage, he asked me if I'd like to spend the weekend in Berchtesgaden. I thought that must be the name of a big track meet down there.

But Dee Beckman told him that I was in training. He said he could understand that because he had to be in shape to run the country. I then asked him for his autograph. Right when he was giving me his autograph some little tiny guy slipped in there and snapped a picture. Well, that Hitler, he jumped right straight up. Dee Beckman whispered to me, "Hey, he just set a world standing high jump record." But it wasn't funny. He was spouting German, and he began to hit and kick that photographer. Then he motioned for his guards to come and get him.

They shook him, and his camera fell out on the floor, and they kicked that around like a soccer ball. Then a couple of them grabbed him and gave him a one, two, three, and threw him out the door and the camera out after him. Then everything returned to normal. I had heard that Hitler could chew carpet and stuff like that. I thought, What are you going to do for an encore after this? Anyway, he wished me well. The next morning that picture was on postcards and sold at the stadium. I got six of them.

Helen Stephens declined the invitation to Berchtesgaden, Hitler's hidden residence, but she did attend a party in Berlin:

I remember that after the Olympics all of the gold medalists were invited to Goebbels's estate along with the upper

400 of Berlin society and the top people of the German army, navy, and air force. They threw a big garden party there for us. They had about seven outdoor dance pavilions and bars with champagne running freely. There were soldiers all over, standing at attention. During the course of the evening, a messenger came up to me and said, "Hermann Goering wants to see you upstairs."

Harriet Bland, a relay runner from St. Louis, and I said, "Hey, this'd be a fun experience to go up there. We won't tell anybody." Well, we went up, and there was a soldier in uniform standing before the door. Now this party was later written up by the press as one of those orgies, and that's what it was. We get inside the door and there's Goering sitting on a great big divan and a couple of gals sitting there in dubious attire. He had a table in front of him, and I knew things weren't according to Hoyle when one of those girls slithered up from under the table. Then I realized this black thing he had on was his kimono, and he was sitting there in his shorts.

And, of course, he gives me the Heil Hitler sign and congratulations. He told me to have a drink and brought the wine over. Well, I thought, I'm not drinking anything here. So I took the wine and toasted with it and set it back, just ceremonial-like. So he says, "You and your friend make yourself comfortable and everything, and if you would like to be more comfortable, I'll have you shown into an adjacent room, and I'll be in to see you later."

I thought, Oh, my God. And Harriet, she's over there talking to somebody. Just then Goering got a phone call, and
a good-looking German officer came up and said, "Would
you like to come over with me and meet so-and-so?" So
we did, and he says, "I don't think you young people
should be here. This is not a proper place, and things will
get out of hand before the evening's over. If you'll bear
with me, I'll introduce you to several well-known officers
who are here." And he introduced me to old World War I
generals, and then he said, "I think you all will be uncomfortable here. We'll gradually work over to the door, if it's
all right with you."

He told us that he didn't approve of what was going to take
place there. We had a hard time catching Harriet and getting her going because she couldn't get it through her head
what was going on. As I got ready to go out the door ol'
Hermann Goering was still on the phone, and he jumps up
and says, "Auf Wiedersehen, Fräulein Stephens." And then
he blew me a kiss—and that's the last I ever saw of him.[13]

Helen Stephens' account of that night in *Tales of Gold* captured the climate of corruption and threat of sexual assaults by
Hitler's closest aides. Eleanor Holm, another American athlete,
was privy to an inside glimpse of partying with Berlin's elite. A
famous swimmer, she had won the gold medal in 1932 for the
backstroke. At the time of the 1936 Games, she held six world
records and was a prominent athlete on the American team. She
had ignored rules of "proper" conduct aboard the ship bound
for Germany, drinking and carousing, according to complaints

of one of the chaperones. Avery Brundage ousted her as a bad example for the American team. Delighting in notoriety, she managed to be highly visible at the Games and was befriended by the United States newspaper entourage.

Holm recalled:

The Germans could not understand anybody being kicked off the team for drinking wine when they had wine on their training tables. I'll never forget when Goering and Hitler said that if I had been a German athlete, the punishment would have come after I had won the gold medal. I later thought, Yeah, probably Buchenwald or some other concentration camp.

Goering was fun. He really did give me a silver swastika, but it isn't silver; it's tarnishing.

. . . I was invited to everything in Berlin, and he [Brundage] would be there, too. He would be so miserable because I was at all these important functions. . . . How dare I be there and take away his thunder?[14]

The Games and celebrations were drawing to a close. Buoyed by splendid achievements, the crowd had an insatiable appetite for every flourish put before them. Helene was to have one more chance to face the spectators who pressed into the huge arena for the formal presentation of medals to the three fencing finalists. When it was their turn, the winners entered the stadium and took their places one behind the other. Ilona Schacherer-Elek, the winner of the gold medal, was in the middle.

The wreaths of leaves in their hair, an homage to the Greek antecedents, were in stark contrast to the elegantly tailored clothing worn by the fencers. Ilona stood at attention, dressed in a white suit, holding the sapling oak tree in her left arm. In front of her, equally sedate in demeanor, stood Ellen, the bronze medalist with the Austrian insignia attached to her dark jacket. Helene stood behind Ilona. A handsome figure dressed in form-fitting white slacks, Helene bore an emblem of the swastika-bearing eagle on her white turtleneck sweater. Her gaze was steely, composed, and resolute. She extended her right arm in a stiff "Heil Hitler" salute. The crowd burst into spontaneous applause.

It seemed a natural thing to do. All the Germans saluted their leader. Helene wanted to leave a lasting impression on the public that she was a true German. Unfortunately, her heartbreaking, chilling gesture was an homage to Hitler. To the Germans it was an exclusive gesture, binding a nation in common cause.

Some reacted with revulsion and horror, including a Jewish classmate of Helene's from the Schillerschule.[15] Most Germans saw her salute as affirmative, a pledge of allegiance to Hitler.

Gretel Bergmann, the Jewish high jumper who had been forced off the German team, answered the question about what her decision would have been had she found herself on the podium standing before thousands of expectant spectators. Would she have made the Nazi salute? Over 60 years after the event Gretl, who had changed her name to Margaret, repudiated Germany, and married Bruno Lambert in the United States, stated, "I ask myself that question every day of my life. I don't know the answer. I might be dead now. There was a terrible climate of unimaginable fear in Germany."

Helene's stance and outstretched arm, poised in the direction

Silver medalist Helene Mayer presents the Nazi salute,
standing behind Ilona Schacherer-Elek, gold medal winner,
cradling her gift of a sapling oak tree

of the Nazi entourage, dominated the scene. Her salute mini-mized Schacherer-Elek's victory. *Hitler über alles* (Hitler above all else) overwhelmed the ceremony.

The Nazis were not conciliatory. There was no news of Helene's request for citizenship; the title "honorary Aryan" never appeared. Doris recalled, "At the end of the Games, we—the German team—were invited into the Reichs-Chancellor's office. 'He' didn't want to come but we talked her into it. She was among us and did not regret it. But she still mourned that little oak tree she never won."

Helene's fixation on the little oak tree is perhaps a metaphor for herself. Once she had been a young sapling, thriving in German soil, sturdy and strong. Then she was shockingly uprooted and tossed aside. What she ignored was the seed from which each oak tree grew. She closed her mind to her Jewish roots, her father, grandparents, great-grandparents, and those who came before them producing generations of offspring who enriched the nation. An oak tree, symbolic of Helene and her Jewish ancestry, could not have been planted in Germany in 1936. It would have withered and died in that toxic place.

A solemn athlete faces an uncertain future

Chapter 12

THE OLYMPIC PAUSE

IN THE LATE AFTERNOON OF SUNDAY, AUGUST 16, 1936, thousands once again crammed into the Olympic Stadium to witness the concluding ceremonies. The Olympic Bell pealed, trumpets blared, and flag-bearers promenaded the field for the last time. Muffled cannon shots could be heard in the distance. It was a solemn moment. Sedate young girls with laurel wreaths in their hair evoked kinship with ancient Greece. A hazy sun sank in the west behind the five Olympic rings, which appeared suspended in air.

Hitler shared the spotlight in the closing ceremonies with the I.O.C. president, Baron de Coubertin, who declared:

The swaying and the struggles of history will continue, but little by little knowledge will replace dangerous ignorance, mutual understanding will soften unthinkable hatreds . . . May the German people and their head be thanked for what they have just accomplished! And you, athletes, remember the sun-kindled fire which has come to you from Olympia to lighten and warm our epoch. Guard it jealously, in the depths of your being in order that it may leap up again on the other side of the world four years hence, when you celebrate the XII Olympiad on the far shores of the great Pacific Ocean.

Hitler's remarks were perfunctory:

I hope that the Berlin Olympic games have assisted in strengthening the Olympic ideals and thereby have helped to form a connecting link between nations . . . you have rendered a signal service to the physical fitness of the human race and the better understanding among peoples.[1]

The Nazis had no intention of going beyond giving lip service to hollow words of brotherhood and democratic values; what followed was a carefully calculated resumption of hostilities in pursuit of their enemies, especially the Jews. The success of the Games inflated Nazi self-esteem and the view of themselves as distinguished warriors. Who could have guessed that de Coubertin's pledge of the next great Olympic Games in 1940, to be held in Tokyo, would never happen? For the second time in the 20th century, countries would be engulfed in a world war.

Some have described the 1936 Games and the period immediately following as the "Olympic Pause," an intermission, a lull between peace and war. During this pause, the Nazis confounded their detractors and reassured their supporters with pious words. In a regime based on hatred, their prattle about brotherly love and human rights was inane but they knew what the world wanted to hear.

Returning athletes were intoxicated by the show in Berlin. A warm welcome, decent accommodations, and superb sports facilities mattered. The political climate was unimportant and of little interest to a self-absorbed athlete, looking for a taste of fame and the hope of immortality. Archie Williams, a gold medalist and one of 10 men who were referred to as "black auxiliaries" by the Nazi press, said:

> I got a big kick out of Germany. Here's a 21-year-old kid who'd never been out of California. Hell, I didn't even know where Germany was. The German people did just what you'd expect. They'd rub our skin to see if it would come off. But the people were themselves. I didn't know that much about Hitler or what he was doing. In fact, as far as I was concerned, they were just friendly, warm people who were happy to have us there.[2]

Echoing the benign view was Forrest "Spec" Towns, another gold medal winner in the 110-meter hurdles, who commented:

> I think Berlin was the first big-time Olympic Games. They really went all out. . . . Of course, I did not participate in the politics of it. I went there to run and do my thing, and that's what I did. I don't think any athletes got involved in the political side of things. If anybody was involved in politics, it had to be the officials of the Olympic Committee.[3]

Berlin was very exciting, recalled John Woodruff, a long-distance runner:

The accommodations they had for us were absolutely superb. We stayed in the Olympic Village right outside of Berlin about 15 miles. Our chef was from the *SS Bremen,* which was an outstanding German luxury liner. The food was excellent and everything was immaculate. The organization was superb. The old-timers who had gone to previous Olympics said the Berlin Games were the best. Hitler really put on a show. It couldn't have been run any better. A lot of people asked me how the German people treated us. They treated us royally. They rolled out the red carpet. They were very friendly, very accommodating, very gracious, very cordial. They were considerate in every respect.

We did see soldiers marching to and fro in the city of Berlin, but we didn't pay any attention to them. Of course, we had heard quite a bit about Hitler. There was a lot of talk about how he was persecuting the Jews. But personally, I wasn't interested in politics, and I think that was the same feeling many of the athletes had. However, we did talk to a young German athlete who visited with us one day in the Olympic Village. We asked him what the Germans thought of Hitler. He spoke English very well and told us that they thought he was a great man because he had done so much for the country from an economic point of view: everyone was working and so forth. He had opened up all of those factories to make war armaments so everybody had a job. They thought that was wonderful.[4]

American dignitaries returning from Berlin assured President Roosevelt, who remained aloof during the Olympic controversy. Said one, "The synagogues were crowded and apparently there is nothing very wrong."[5] In New York City, Brundage addressed a German-American Day rally at Madison Square Garden and announced, "No country since ancient Greece has displayed a more truly national interest in the Olympic spirit than you can find in Germany today."

In Germany, the Olympic spirit was sorely tested. It was indeed true that extensive persecutions against Jews and other enemies of the state had decreased during the lull, but there were tragic casualties. Captain Wolfgang Fuerstner, who oversaw the Olympic Village planning and construction and was a director of Germany's athletic program, was suddenly dismissed from the army and removed from his post.[6] It had been discovered that he was partly Jewish. He continued to serve as second-in-command at the Olympic Village.

A week after the Games, following a banquet held for his replacement, Captain Fuerstner shot and killed himself with a single bullet. The German press was ordered to report his death as an auto accident. Lewald, who so tenaciously defended the regime's policy toward German-Jewish athletes, was unceremoniously relieved of his duties because he was half-Jewish. The public humiliation of these obedient bureaucrats sent a chilling message to vulnerable others who had loyally served the regime.

Luckily, Helene had options. Had her fondest dreams come true, a gold medal coupled with restoration of citizenship, she may have been sorely tempted to remain in Germany, protected by an "honorary Aryan status." Despite the failure to win gold, her six-month stay in Germany was a seductive interlude. There was no evidence of any further discussion of Helene's bid for renewed citizenship. Germany was a perilous place for a "half-Jew" subject to the Nuremberg Laws. To be on the safe side, a return to the United States seemed the wisest course. It was best to wait and see what the future held, so Helene left Germany to return to California.

By this time the racial laws were firmly entrenched. Helene's younger brother, Ludwig, was not allowed to enter a university. Her older brother, Eugen, a second-year medical student, was forced to terminate his training. He worked as a laborer in a scheme of coerced "community service." In 1936, Helene failed in her effort to help him obtain a visa to Peru.

Helene's easygoing ability to bounce back served her well in this unstable state of affairs. The resumption of her life at Mills College was agreeable, but after the excitement of the Games, teaching fencing and Beginning German to a coterie of female college students seemed confining. In contrast to Berlin, Mills was a backwater, a quiet, dull place, not up to the expectations of famous athletes like Helene, but at least she was out of harm's way. Mills was a haven, a place of refuge for Helene to recover from the exciting, tumultuous months in Germany.

She was forced to contemplate two conflicting self-images. In Germany, she was no longer treated as the star she had been, her reputation sullied by her "shameful heritage." At Mills, she was greeted as a returning heroine and was dubbed Mills' "ambassador" to the Olympics. It was an ironic twist of fate for the fencer, who had once been the toast of her country and yearned to become a member of the German diplomatic corps, to be seen as a representative of a small American college.

The front-page story in the *Mills College Weekly* on September 22, 1936, read: "Helene Mayer is Interviewed on Olympic Games Experience." In part, the article said:

"An interview about the Olympic games? But there's so much to tell, where shall I start?" . . . As most Mills College students know, Helene (we're going to be familiar) set out in February for New York, where she was to train for a week at the New York Fencers Club. En route she stopped in Chicago and met President Aurelia Henry Reinhardt, who assured her that a teaching position at Mills would be waiting for her in the fall. At the time of her departure from Mills, she had not known whether she would return or not. . . .

From the moment of her arrival in Germany, Helene was treated as any other member of the German team. . . . For a time she lived in Königstein near Frankfurt to train. Later she continued her training in camps both in the North and South of Germany. During the preliminary tournaments at the training camps, Helene soon established herself as the best fencer on the German team. Although the members of the team were provided with Hungarian and French coaches, Helene applied the adjective "ghastly" to them and received additional instruction from her own Italian fencing master, Tagliabo.

Berlin was highly decorated in honor of the Games and

great excitement reigned in the stadium with Hitler watching every day and many influential German officials as well . . . She met many of the American athletes and saw a great deal of Helen Stephens, the famous sprinter . . . Through elimination, the eight best fencers were chosen from the original forty-five competitors. Judging was very hard; for many of the fencers were not at all lady-like and fenced in a rather wild manner. Helene, however used her customary elegant style of fencing and lost the finals by only one touch to a representative of Hungary.

With the customary ceremony, the three winners of the fencing events were awarded their medals by the president of the International Olympic Committee and laurel wreaths were put on their heads while everyone in the huge stadium stood in recognition of their accomplishments. Besides her silver Olympic medal, the fencer from Mills collected several others, one being the Berlin medal and another the Olympic remembrance medal presented to all active participants and having the Olympic Bell with the words, "I call the youth of the world" engraved on it. Another trophy in her collection is the honorary award given her as the most elegant fencer and having a gold medal in the center.

In addition to her medals, Helene returned with several good looking suits, sports outfits, and fencing costumes which the German government generously gave to its athletes. In addition she brought back beautiful scarves and pins given her by the German government and several fine leather bags. To quote Helene, she "collected more stuff this year than ever before."

The cheerful, extraordinarily superficial interview Helene gave to the paper could certainly have been prepared just as easily by a Nazi official or diplomat. She was treated generously and fairly by the government—she received gifts and medals, "lots of stuff." Her only criticism had to do with the ineptitude of the foreign fencing coaches. She provided no context, not a hint of the social and racial issues plaguing her life. She expressed no indignation about her unmet demands for citizenship and lack of recognition by German newspapers. She avoided any hint of disappointment in the outcome of the most important fencing match of her life. Helene omitted mention of her "Heil Hitler" salute on the podium.

As to her off-hand remark about collecting "more stuff," the "stuff" she really sought to recover was not fine leather handbags or beautiful scarves, but citizenship. The interview ended with recognition of the support Helene had received from Mills students.

Helene was not forgotten by her American friends. She received several hundred letters, a hundred telegrams and many calls at her home on Königstein where her hospitable mother entertained her friends. A great deal of her time was spent with Becky Bacon, who received her M.A. at Mills in 1935. Another Mills student whom Helene saw was Tinka Strauss.

It was Tinka who wrote in the *Mills College Weekly* extolling the many pleasures of serving the German nation in a summer work camp. Helene found succor in the hospitality of her American friends. She clung to the outpouring of affection and unquestioning support that helped to sustain her in the ambivalent return to the United States. Lacking strong moral convictions, she held no critical commitment to political causes or social issues. Her lack of interest fostered an adaptive stance, a chameleon-like quality that allowed her to be pliable and changeable, depending on circumstances.

Certainly, fear for her family's future must have influenced her self-censored, sanitized version of Third Reich hegemony. But Helene had lost sight of moral issues. Rather than challenge Nazi ideology, she stood to one side at a time the regime was plotting the fate of endless enemies.

Helene was back in America but was it by choice? Had the second part of her "bargain" with Germany been kept, her citizenship would have been reinstated. Would she have remained in Germany or returned to the United States, unable to live with what Germany was becoming? What is known is that in the events of the previous two years, 1934-1936, Helene was cagey but single-minded in her desire to fence at the Olympics and in this, she succeeded. What is clear in retrospect is that she handled the predicament not as an identified Jew nor as a person appalled by Nazi rule, but as an ambitious athlete doing whatever was necessary to achieve her goal.

In October 1936, an announcement appeared in the *Weekly* that Helene would address the college for the first time since her return from Germany. The article stated:

In addition to speaking of the training, the provisions made for the athletes, and the sympathies prevalent at the

1936 Olympiad, the speaker whose enthusiasm as well as the number of her trophies and souvenirs has just been increased by the arrival of her trunk from home, will also include comments on the original Olympics held in Greece, the games played, the customs observed, and the significance of the Olympiads to the ancient Greeks.[7]

Here again, Helene chose to keep her remarks noncontroversial and bland. She didn't dare speak on the subject of the significance of the 1936 Games to current Germany. There was not the slightest indication of any dangers posed by Nazi ideology. There was no further elucidation on "sympathies prevalent" at the Games. A student who was present at the lecture recalled that Helene casually called Hitler "a cute little man."[8]

Indeed, Hitler was short, of unimposing stature, particularly to Helene who favored tall men. But why describe this fearsome dictator in such an innocuous and offhand manner? Perhaps an attempt by Helene to humanize Hitler, rendering him harmless by diminishing and denying his awesome power? Such a "cuddly" man could not be held responsible for Helene's misfortunes. It was perhaps an unconscious attempt to project Hitler's image as a benign father figure to the audience at Mills and indeed to Helene herself. A more nuanced approach would have been appropriate; somewhere in her remarks, public or private, one expected words of warning and concern that never came.

Helene's prodigious reserves of good humor and nonchalance were sorely tested by the disappointments she had suffered in Germany. The flight from reality and the need to present a gracious, easygoing public facade gave way to some agitated behavior in private. The German Department had undergone a modest change in Helene's absence. She returned in September to find that the new head of the department was Dr. Bernhard Blume, a German educator and playwright from Berlin. He was an anti-fascist married to a Jewish educator who arrived with their children for the fall semester. Dr. Blume's young son Frank recalled "tearful scenes" between Helene and his father.

He also remembered dinner table conversations that included talks of Helene's tardiness. Sometimes she even missed class, and began to develop habits of heavy cigarette smoking and beer drinking. Dr. Blume was critical of her informal teaching style, scolding her for her "lazy ways." Their uneasy relationship was exacerbated by Dr. Blume's strong anti-Nazi sentiments compared to Helene's passivity, but they did manage to fashion a working relationship. Frank Blume adored Helene. He said, "She was a big, beautiful amazon . . . very warm and tender to me and my brother."

If Dr. Blume was dissatisfied and had more energetic plans for the German department, Helene's students were perfectly happy with her informal classes. "She wanted to make teaching fun. She was not a serious professor . . . She only wanted to have a happy class" were the recollections of students. She called her amalgam of English and German words *die shainster language* (the prettiest language). She called her dog "Good Boychen." Another student remembered, "She seemed in a good mood all the time."

The fencing students remembered her as "a magnificent fencer . . . so much energy . . . even though she could cream us, she still fenced with us." "We went to a sporting goods shop and bought fencing foils for seven dollars each." Many students did not know why she was in the United States—"I'm not sure what brought her to America . . . Her father somehow was involved . . . Somebody told me she was partly Jewish." Other students reported that Helene "spoke little about her family, particularly when she returned from the Olympics . . . she didn't talk about politics."

"Helene was a small group person. She liked to be surrounded by no more than eight to 10 people. She didn't get involved with the world situation." Neither did the students who described some of their own attitudes and the campus social scene. "We were a bunch of stupid girls playing bridge. . . ." "We went blithely on with our classes. . . ." "The school was like a nunnery. . . ." "There was a lot of intimacy and bonding at Mills, no place to go. . . ." "We didn't listen to the radio, we ignored the world out there. . . ." "I don't remember any newspapers in the dorm."

There was not much news of German intransigence in the waning weeks of 1936. During this Olympic Pause, if the students had read a newspaper, they would have found little information about the recently ended Games. Journalists who had energetically covered them went home. The Games were over and done. Helene no longer commanded the attention of Olympic fans or journalists. There was little curiosity to follow up the business of the notorious "deal" that Helene had tried to make with the Nazi government, the unfulfilled promise of citizenship in exchange for her participation in the Games.

In a radio speech, Thomas Mann, one of the most illustrious authors in the world and a German who left his country after Hitler's rise to power, criticized Helene.[9] He was living in Southern California when Helene returned to Mills. He would have preferred her to use her celebrity and influence to warn the world of the dangers of Nazi philosophy. Perhaps as a fellow German, he felt compelled to chastise her for her endorsement and seeming support of the Nazi regime.

After the accelerated tempo and excitement of Berlin, a cooling-down period in California gave Helene a chance to review the experience. She wrote a letter to her friends on the German Olympic team. The letter revealed far more of her feelings than she had shared with friends and students at Mills. Doris Runzheimer, one of Helene's Olympics roommates, and other athletes received a handwritten letter from Helene in November 1936, three months after the Games. A jumble of emotions: affection, anger, blame, loneliness, and resignation were disclosed. She wrote:

Dear Molly, Gisela, Tilly, Dolly, Doris, "viscur," "Mensch Käthe," Elfriede and however you are called:

I am sitting here in my room and outside we have clear-blue skies and California warmth. I have put aside all the papers that I have to correct and now I have to have my chitchat with you. Maybe you have already forgotten me, but I promised to write and here is my letter.

I think back on those days in Germany sooo often. You cannot imagine how vividly the memory stays with me. My trip to Germany lies long in the past and I am back to my university life in America. Here nobody is interested in the Olympic Games. "That is over," other sensations like strikes, presidential elections, football games follow each other—hence there is no room in the newspapers. But it's always like that here in America.

Although I have a ton of work to do, I always find a quarter of an hour during which I think back on my splendid days in Germany, especially with you guys. I don't want to sing anybody's praises, but I really mean it, when I count the days that I was able to spend with you in good camradery among the most wonderful in my life . . . you were all so decent and good to me and I will never forget that. I can thank you from my heart only in clumsy words, but I hope that you understand me.

I am gone from home now for three months . . . home was Königstein in Taunus at mom's . . . and a lot has happened. I almost broke my neck in an automobile accident—I was driving by myself and collided with a truck. I had lots of cuts on my arms, legs and in my face and my chest was pretty crushed. The car is a wreck—it's all very awful, expensive and nerve-wracking. But over here people don't show a lot of consideration for private matters like that. You are sutured, your ribs are put back together and then work goes on. I am a German instructor here, which means I am teaching girls (18 to 24 years old) German grammar and I also give lectures: German literature from the Song of Hildebrand to the present. There are approximately 500 students at Mills College who all live here. It's a kind of university–boarding home. We live in six big buildings, so-called "dormitories," where every girl has her own room. We eat together in a big cafeteria: a lot of singing, a lot of noise and not particularly good food.

Aside from my duties as a German instructor I also have to watch the girls in my building. They have to be inside at a certain hour at night and they have to ask my permission, if they want to leave for the weekend. Because the age difference is not very big, it is somewhat hard for me to get the necessary respect, but it now works fabulously. We get along very well. We often have a "German meal," where only German is spoken. We have advent wreaths, sing German Christmas songs as often as possible and have a big Christmas party, which consists of a nativity play and a banquet. I'm already tearing my hair because Joseph says his lines again and again with the same awful pronunciation and Mary rocks her baby with such true American energy that the cradle almost tips over. I hope that they will get it right by Christmas!!

Here in America the press denigrated the Olympics on purpose. It's all propaganda against Germany! But it didn't do them much good because all of us, and by that I mean the American Olympic athletes, worked against that. I have given a lot of speeches at clubs, universities and once even on the radio (National Broadcasting Station) and I let them have it! Those wind-bags who still cannot get over the fact that the Olympics in Berlin were the highlight of all the Olympics. They still go on about the case of Elinor Holm, but it doesn't really matter to us.

So time goes by with a lot of work and homesickness. Sometimes I look at a world map and I see in horror how far away San Francisco really is from Germany! Just take a look for yourselves!

Will we see each other again in the future? I don't know. All I know is that I want to come back to Germany, but there surely is no room for me . . . I am one of those souls who was hit by a harsh fate. I love Germany just as much as you do and I feel and think just as German as you do!

I read about Käthe's fine position in Dresden. Wow, my congratulations! I am happy for you. And now gather up all your energy and drop me a postcard for Christmas. I wish you all the best!

In loyal comradery—
yours Helene
Enclosed a few stamps for Käthe!

The letter tells a story of an unwilling exile who returns to a strange country, the United States, which is welcoming but still foreign. She thinks back on "the splendid days in Germany" but reels from the shock of her recent traumatic experiences there. She angrily defends Germany, her country. She is on a self-imposed mission to uphold its reputation. Thoughts of rage and disillusion with her plight must be suppressed in order to soften the wounding reflections. Helene fiercely defends her patriotism. She never mentions Hitler, Nazism, or the changes in Germany.

All she proclaims is her love of country. An indispensable identity is embedded in her psyche and will not be dislodged. Her letter can be understood as a plea to her teammates that she remains worthy of citizenship. But the promise was broken and Helene fled to the United States and takes on the "mantle of

German-ness" not the "mantle of Nazism" in the letter to her friends. Helene takes a morally lethal step in embracing her oppressor, blind and resistant to the injustices that had been heaped upon her. She ends with the plaintive cry of her innocence. Her "harsh fate," because she is partially Jewish, is intolerable. Perhaps the sharp rebuke from Thomas Mann added to her defensive posture.

According to victimology theory, as situations worsen, victims have diminished capacity to acknowledge the actual enemy. Denial of corruption and evil becomes greater as powerful defensive posturing erases rational judgment. The victim, Helene, is not only alienated from her country; she is alienated from herself. Aharon Appelfeld, a writer and analyst of the profound effects of relentless Nazi propaganda against Jews, wrote of the "twin impulses" to run away from and to run toward an abuser. In a life-saving gesture, Helene literally "ran away" from the abuser by seeking sanctuary in the United States. Psychologically, she "ran towards" the abuser, in her irrational need to support the powerful victimizer. (Whether she made the public appearances she claimed she made is unknown. What emerges at this point is her obsessive urge to promote Germany.) Nazi propaganda confirmed and made final the loathing many Jews felt for themselves and each other.

Primo Levi, a concentration camp survivor and prolific author after the Nazi era, described the psychological as well as physical hazards of victimhood. He saw the unparalleled trauma as a ghastly test of human behavior in a state of shock. Victims often feel compelled to become accomplices in the acts against them . . . a morally and ultimately physically destructive process. Feelings of humiliation and self-hatred are turned inward and together form a bond that blocks the victim from rational responses. Only those with powerful moral beliefs have a chance of discovering the truth and labeling the real enemy.

In the letter Helene sent to her German friends she characterized a Germany that was misunderstood. She wrote, "It's all propaganda against Germany," and referred to "those wind-bags who still cannot get over the fact that the Olympics in Berlin were the highlight of all the Olympics." Public sentiment as well seemed to accept a more benign view of Germany. For a brief period of time, the Olympic Pause seduced a public that was puzzled and too willing to be led astray. Transfixed by the action on the playing fields, a grudging admiration for German accomplishments gripped viewers worldwide. A meticulously arranged Act I, the Olympic Games in Berlin with their unforgettable images of human strength and purpose mesmerized the onlookers. The spectators loved it. The athletes felt triumphant. Olympic fervor was inescapable.

The year 1936 was crucial in Nazi ascendancy. The Olympic Pause was a comforting interlude that ended the year with false hopes of a peaceable world landscape. But the curtain was about to rise on Act II. Helene was no longer a unique victim. She was also an onlooker of increasing German atrocities. Soon, Helene's actions would begin to reflect an individual who was no longer in denial. She would reach the point where she would question, but not yet condemn, the horrific policies of a brutal regime.

"Jews are not wanted here"—
a dreadful preamble to their fate in Germany and Europe

Chapter 13

A DOOMED DECADE

In high spirits, Helene returned to California after winning the U.S. National Championship for the third consecutive year. In early May 1937, Helene wrote an article for the *Mills College Weekly* that said:

> I cannot remember any trip of the last four years which was not a hurried enterprise; this time it was a 13 day trip to New York to compete in the national fencing championships as a representative of California.

> A short sojourn for a "normal" person in New York must be wonderful—plays, concerts, exhibitions, museums, parties—but I have not come to New York to "have a good time," while the girls at Mills went on with their work. I had a national fencing tournament before me and with noblesse oblige I had to renounce all the worldly

pleasures of New York. I spent most of my time at the Fencers' Club with Professor Rene Pichart, who had told me a few years ago that my lungs were as heavy as a sac de farine [a sack of flour] and this time I was most eager for him not to repeat that compliment.

Before the training, I could of course dispose of my time in intelligent ways—tea parties in the very luxurious apartment in the St. Regis where I stayed with the famous aviatrix and friend of our Dr. "B" [Blume], Antonie Strassman; walks along the famous avenues with their fine shops, one play, "Yes, My Darling Daughter," and in order to be very strong for the fight, food in Italian, Chinese, Russian and French places.

The tournament itself was a very arduous affair. It lasted from 8:00 a.m. until after midnight . . . There is always a certain tension and strain . . . but I did win without a default having given 65 touches and received 14 during the whole meet. The joy among my friends, especially my "rooting section" composed of Connie Dean, Al Snyder, Pacific Coast men's foil champion . . . Ursula Pauli's parents, and an old friend of mine from Italy . . . afterwards we had a big celebration.

. . . I packed my things and was about to leave New York the next morning. But suddenly an invitation from the Mills Alumnae of New York reached me asking me to listen to the Eighty-Fifth Anniversary broadcast and therefore I postponed the trip for a few hours . . . It was a wonderful experience to be so far away from Mills but still have the feeling to "belong" so very much, while the President's voice sounded clear through the space!

When Pat Green met me at the 16th Street station with her newly washed and shiny car, my first question was, "Did I miss something on campus?" No, it didn't seem so. Everything had gone smoothly, especially my classes in German and fencing.

It is hard to believe that this was the same Helene who had written the angry and disheartened letter to her friends in Germany six months earlier. The customary pleasures of fencing soothed and refreshed her as nothing else could. A smaller audience, but she basked in the attention of her celebrity status in the United States. Like the voluptuary she was, Helene took unabashed delight in the urbane atmosphere of New York. She made sure to acknowledge Mills' anniversary and in a flattering aside, mentioned the worthy folks who supported her. The Berlin Olympics could have occurred on another planet.

Cheered by her success in New York, Helene returned to Mills in May. She directed a local Bay Area fencing tournament. The *Weekly* reported:

During and after the competition the fencers were the envy of passersby as they celebrated the final meet with iced tea, cookies and ice cream, distributed by Helene Mayer. The center of attraction . . . a chocolate cake decorated with pipe-cleaner fencers representing Helene Mayer and Hazel Murray.

The gossip columnist chimed in:

We used to think we'd like to dence (poetic license)
Now we wish we could fence.

On account of the tea party that Helene prepared for her
sword sharks the other day. There it was all laid out under
the big, cool tree behind the gym.

Innocent fun! No tournament was too trifling or unimportant for Helene: provide a challenging opponent, a *salle d'arme,*
and she was there.

The conditions in Germany continued in a downward spiral
and were noted in the Mills newspaper. A front-page article entitled "Czechs are Victims of Nazi Propaganda" reported the
spread of Germany's threat to its neighboring countries. Student
organizations, frightened by the implications of such provoca-
tions, pleaded for world peace and sought to galvanize public
opinion to assure peace and "outlaw war."

A question posed by anxious students was published in the
Weekly: "Do you believe that it is the duty of our government to
protect American property, citizens, and commerce, even if such
a defense requires the sending of an army to fight on foreign soil?"
Questions like this were being raised on many college campuses
and in public debates throughout America. Although Germany
was not named directly, there was awareness of the growing menace of a restless nation, anxious to pursue policies which seemed
bereft of rational political and economic considerations.

Helene decided to visit her family again in the summer of
1937, a year after the Olympics. She traveled by train to Detroit

where she boarded a steamer for Montreal and then sailed on a freighter across the Atlantic. After landing in Antwerp, she headed home where an unexpected invitation from the International Fencing Federation to fence in Paris awaited her. Two days after she arrived in Germany, Helene was off to Paris and after three days of preliminary bouts, she qualified for the final matches. Seven of the female fencers, almost the same group that competed in Berlin at the Olympics, participated.

In Paris, Helene again fenced against Ilona Schacherer-Elek, the gold medalist, and Ellen Preis, the bronze medalist, from the 1936 Games. In highly exciting matches, Helene defeated both of them and won the world championship. It was a remarkable comeback. She collected elaborate medals and a silver cup presented by the French women's magazine, *Marie Claire*. Her victory received wide publicity in France.

Helene returned to Germany for a joyous celebration with her family. When she arrived at the Frankfurt train station, she asked a friend anxiously, "What is written in the press?" The reply was, "Not a word." "Then I have to remain in America after all," was her inescapable conclusion, acknowledgment that Germany had forsaken her.[1] Her Paris triumph was her last on European soil.

Still caught up in a whirl of fencing, Helene left the freighter carrying her back from Europe for a stopover in Canada before making her way west to California. Aboard ship, she had passed the time fencing with a male Swedish gymnast who had won an Olympic medal in 1912. In Montreal, honored by the Canadian Fencing Federation, she fenced in exhibition matches at the Canadian German Club. From the start of her career, Helene took every opportunity to compete against men. She loved the challenge and was well aware that these mixed bouts enhanced her reputation.

A reporter for a Montreal newspaper described her as "a champion at fencing and good nature. Suntanned from days on a windswept ocean, Helene Mayer descended upon us a vision in blue." Helene was her publicly delightful self, extolling the British fencers who sent her flowers. She said, "When a woman sends you flowers it is a sincere tribute." She answered the reporter's questions about the dangers of injury for fencers. Up went a blue sleeve and a left arm carrying a scar. "Got that in an epee bout when the blade struck where my jacket was too thin." Her eyes sparkled. "Do not let them tell you our sport is without its thrills. It can be killing!" She traveled to Detroit to pick up a new Ford coupe for the cross-country drive back to Mills and arrived on Registration Day. Helene surmised that her life must go on in the United States at Mills. There was, indeed, "no place" for her in Germany. Helene would have to make her peace with America.

Her stay in California took on an air of permanency. Soon after her return in the fall of 1937, Helene moved into a modest cottage near the Mills campus. Although some students recalled it looking "temporary," it was to be her home for the many remaining years she lived in California. She settled in with her books, trophies, mementos, and photographs, including one photo of Adolf Hitler shaking her hand after the 1936 Games.

She entertained students and friends, speaking German, eating German food, singing German songs. The language and culture of her youth were embedded in her private life. Her zest for life and capacity for fun enchanted her students. She was downhearted when mail arrived from Germany. In 1937 Helene started the process of becoming an American citizen. A close friend who knew her at Scripps and Mills recalled accompanying her to the U.S. Immigration Office in San Bernardino, a town near her friend's home, to pick up the papers. "She told me she wanted to remain in America—those were her first papers."[2] However, she let the process languish until 1940 when Nazi atrocities became unbearable.

As 1937 came to an end, the situation in Germany deteriorated further. All Jews had to assume a "new" middle name, Israel for men and Sarah for women, an edict to strip Jews of their individuality and personal distinctiveness.[3] By the end of that year, Jewish professionals, civil servants, actors, musicians, and journalists had lost their livelihoods. They were destitute and unemployable in Germany.

Businesses owned by Jews were confiscated. Initially, there were crude attempts to have the transfers of businesses to Aryans appear as if they were voluntary acts. This subterfuge gave way as more businesses were expropriated by the state. In 1938, every Jew had to report and assess all his domestic and foreign property. Accelerated confiscations coupled with loss of employment emasculated the Jewish population. All Jews were forced to return their passports in exchange for a special identity card, imprinted with a large "J." Jewish magazines and newspapers were banned.

Once her position at Mills was secure, Helene exhibited her independent and daring behavior, at odds with the "good girl" atmosphere at Mills. "She did things no one else did," recalled one student.

Helene was chaperone for a ski weekend. When we sat around an evening fire, one fellow kept asking Helene Mayer how well she knew a certain acquaintance and kept "having in." Finally she said, "Well, I didn't sleep with him." I was very embarrassed by the answer. In those days, one did not speak openly about such intimate matters . . . she certainly was ahead of her times.[4]

She also balked at some of the expected behavior of a "proper" faculty member. She avoided Dr. Reinhardt's weekly inspirational talks that faculty members were expected to attend, garbed in appropriate academic gowns. Another student recollected, "Helene wanted us to do well on final exams. She gave us the answers." She served beer to her guests even though it was against college rules. She permitted herself the freedom and an acceptable degree of rebelliousness that usually charmed and often shocked her audience. Her behavior was in marked contrast to the German culture, where restraint, submission, and obedience to authority figures were the norm.

In spring 1938, Leni Riefenstahl, the famed German filmmaker who had directed the masterpiece *Olympia* two years before at the Berlin Games, visited the United States to promote her film. It was scheduled for release in April to mark Hitler's 49th birthday. Hitler had praised it "as a unique and incomparable glorification of the strength and beauty of our party." The Nazis believed there was a wide audience for the film in the United States.

At this time, a number of private fencing clubs flourished in San Francisco. The studios of Erich Funke, an Austrian emigré, were the best-known. Helene began fencing in one of his studios, where she met the best amateur fencers in the Bay Area. They provided the competition and fun she craved, away from the well-intentioned but awkward Mills students. Here she met Arthur Lane, a young, talented fencer who recalled meeting Helene for the first time in Funke's studio in 1937:

> One evening we hear this song in German being sung by some female climbing the stairs and Erich's ears sort of pointed and his face sort of glowed, and in walked Helene Mayer![5]

Arthur gleefully described going to her cottage to deliver a specially made guard for her foil:

> I was to meet the great Helene in a different place! It was a bit different from just walking up to her on the strip, fencing with her. Here I was, meeting her as a human being, a private person.

> So I knock on the door and here's Helene in the dirtiest old work clothes I'd ever seen. She was busy, standing on top of a very short stepladder washing the ceiling! I told her, "you don't have to wash the ceiling before you paint it. Just put two coats on." I said, "stop!" So I was able to give the great Helene Mayer a command—stop. As far as I know, that's what she did.[6]

Arthur was stunned by her fencing prowess—"beautiful, classic actions"—"very distinct"—"She was never off target." She dominated the field; her defensive and offensive thrusts "were just so clear." He had vague memories of whispered talks about the '36 Olympics and Helen's attempts to raise money to enter tournaments. He recalled Helene never wanted to speak about the '36 Games and how she came to participate. "She was bitter about it." He described Leni Riefenstahl's visit to Funke's studio to meet the fencers, and especially to be introduced to Helene:

A whole group of German-speaking visitors came clomping up the stairs, in the door, clicking heels whenever they were introduced, monocles falling off on their little ribbons, and Helene introducing people. They had been lined up more or less according to rank. But all the fencers were in one group at the end of the line. Here we were being introduced, everyone by name until they got to the fencers and I was the next one, and Helene said grandly, "and the rest are fencers." So I wasn't introduced to Leni Riefenstahl.[7]

In the summer of 1938, Helene visited Germany for the last time before the onset of World War II. European fencing tournaments did not lure her back to Germany. She came to see her family. Helene received ongoing letters from her mother and friends and she was aware that the situation in Germany was explosive and unpredictable.

Helene's brothers were increasingly at risk. Eugen, her elder brother, had Nazi sympathies but was still subject to the Nuremberg Laws. There is a possibility that Eugen may have received help from Reinhard Heydrich, an uncompromising Nazi dubbed "the Blonde Beast" who rose to become chief of the

Gestapo, the secret police.[8] Fencing was Heydrich's lifelong passion and he became acquainted with Eugen through fencing clubs. There was talk he protected some German fencers who were considered Jews.[9] Whether Heydrich had a role in helping Eugen remains unknown. (Heydrich was shot to death in May 1942, near Prague, by two assassins flown from London by the Czech government-in-exile.) There was also hearsay regarding Helene. It was said, but never substantiated, that Heydrich had dispatched two emissaries to the Bay Area to convince Helene to enter the '36 Games.

Two months before Helene's visit in May, the Jews of Frankfurt am Main were subjected to a day of intimidation and humiliation modeled on a similar outrage to Austrian Jews soon after the German takeover. In Vienna, Jews had been dragged to an amusement park where they were forced to eat grass, climb trees, twitter like birds, and then run around in circles until they collapsed.[10] The day in the Frankfurt park was dubbed "pleasure hours" by the Nazis, reducing human beings to a state of tortured animals.

Helene returned to California alone. She told friends that her mother had chosen to remain in Germany, fearing change and the loss of her pension. Helene expressed concern for the *kleine* Ludwig, "young Ludwig," but no arrangements were made for either brother to leave Germany. The final incident that ensured Helene's residence in the United States occurred in November 1938. A shameless display of hatred against Jews resulted in a "tidal wave of terror." It was called *Kristallnacht,* the "night of glass," when the Jewish community in Germany went up in flames. On November 7, 1938, a Polish-Jewish student assassinated Ernst vom Rath, a minor German Embassy official stationed in Paris. The following day, his death turned him into a Nazi martyr, providing the justification to arouse assembled mobs throughout Germany.

Goebbels, the minister of propaganda, became the advocate for mob violence and called for "spontaneous" demonstrations against Jews as revenge for vom Rath's death. Tons of shattered glass littered German streets as synagogues, businesses, and homes were set on fire. Jews were manhandled in the streets. In a few days, the pogrom had reached a peak of destruction. Over 7,000 Jewish businesses went up in flames, thousands were hurt and taunted, and more than 100 Jews died. Photographs of the explosion of demented violence were seen all over the world. The photographs were so compelling one could almost hear the glass breaking and feel the shards underfoot. The Nazis showed utter disdain for world opinion.

The fires died down and tempers cooled, but the government reissued a torrent of edicts. A punitive fine of 1 billion marks, called a contribution, was placed on the Jewish community to pay for the destruction they had caused! Jews were barred from all public places, including theaters, beaches, resorts, and sleeping car compartments on trains. All Jewish children remaining in German schools were expelled. The government reserved the right to impose curfew restrictions. Jews were forbidden to sell any goods or services in Germany.

Over 30,000 Jewish men were arrested and sent to concentration camps. The outbreak of World War II on September 3, 1939, ended the possibilities of escape from Germany. "In 1938 'emigration' was an euphemism for 'expulsion.' Once war began, 'evacuation' became an euphemism for 'deportation,' which in turn, signified 'transportation to a place of death.'"[11]

What remained of the Jewish population in Germany was hopelessly trapped.

Helene's mother's house was searched by the Gestapo; she believed that a copy of the photograph of Hitler congratulating Helene at the 1936 Games kept the police at bay. In California, Helene removed that photo from its prominent place in her house. A student recalled, "the photo disappeared."

Helene now began the citizenship process. She had a job, a small house, friends, some celebrity status, and fencing opportunities. Outside of her concern for her family, she was not one to wring her hands over the fate of thousands of trapped Jews. She had a safe niche; her survival would be ensured if she remained in the United States. Helene took steps to put Germany behind her, to enjoy the good life in California. She began to rejuvenate her social contacts with people outside of her "coterie of girls" at Mills.

She had met Imogen Cunningham, a famous portrait photographer, when she arrived at Mills. Imogen's husband, Roi Partridge, taught in the Fine Arts Department at the college. By the time Helene became acquainted with Cunningham, the photographer had produced a large body of commissioned portraits of people in the arts, music, literature, and sports. Always looking for subjects who projected strong and emphatic personalities, Cunningham found Helene a winning subject. One of her most splendid portraits, taken of Helene in 1935, compels the viewer's eyes to meet the fencer's in a direct, steady gaze. The protective mask and foil seem to be an extension of the fencer although the face-shaped mask, shrouded in mesh, alongside the subject alludes to concealed aspects of the fencer's persona.

Helene and Imogen became close friends. Helene was a frequent guest at Imogen's parties. Rondal Partridge, Imogen's son, remembered Helene as an ebullient, saucy woman: "Once, she arrived at my mother's house and pulled up her dress and said—'California is marvelous—my tummy is brown.'"[12] (She was referring to a sunburn.) Helene smuggled a German camera for Imogen into the United States after her last visit to Germany. In 1938, Helene sat for one of Imogen's series of her "bohemian" friends.

In 1938, at one of Imogen's gatherings, Helene met Joseph Sinel, a talented and quirky industrial designer and artist from New Zealand who immigrated to the United States in 1917 and moved to San Francisco. He had lived in the Southwest and Montana, where he had "nearly married three or four squaws."[13] She found him attractive, despite a 20-year disparity in their ages and his disinterest in sports. Both self-centered and absorbed in their careers, they were lovers for 10 years but never married. Helene called him "My Joe" and they were a conspicuous couple driving around on the Mills campus, Joe puffing a cigar, Helene looking svelte sitting close to him. They vacationed in the Sierra, where Joe owned a summer cabin. As the likelihood of war increased, Rondal Partridge recalled dinner conversations about world events: "We were critical of Germany in front of Helene. Once she said, 'Remember, not all Germans are like Hitler.'"

Fencing, a healer and source of satisfaction to Helene, occupied a great deal of her time and remained an essential part of her life. She also had a great interest in promoting the sport. In 1938, she won the U.S. National Championship for the fourth year in a row. Expenses incurred by entering competitions were almost always assumed by the athletes involved. As an amateur athlete, Helene did not earn her living as a fencer. Corporate sponsorship was virtually unknown at that time. Like other contenders, Helene relied on the hospitality of interested fans and supporters when she traveled to different cities.

Hitler's meticulous plans for the dismemberment of Europe began in earnest in 1939. World War II was on the horizon. The circumscribed war against Jews in Germany was almost completed. Between 1933 and 1939, over 400 edicts eradicating Jewish life in Germany had been passed by the Reichstag.[14] The Jews left were those who could not or would not leave because of poverty, ill health, or denial of the dangers they faced. In the aftermath of *Kristallnacht* and preparation for war, avenues for escape were virtually closed off. They would soon be dealt with. Now Europe awaited its fate as Germany's craving to create new colonies and prepare new killing fields to destroy all European Jews fueled invasions into neighboring countries. Hitler called his enterprise "the great racial war," exposing his dream of eliminating "alien" populations.

The scope of German military ambitions was met with alarmed concern in the United States. Victims who could still get out scurried about to find avenues of escape from deadly entrapment in Europe. In 1939, a figure from the past, Hans Halberstadt, re-entered Helene's life. He was a member of a prominent Offenbach Jewish family that had prospered in the leather tanning trade. With the help of influential Nazis, who shared his interest in fencing, he had been released from the Dachau concentration camp.

He made his way to Amsterdam for his journey to the U.S. on the very day—September 1, 1939—that Germany invaded

Poland. Penniless, he managed to reach San Francisco to join his sister and brother, who had earlier fled Germany. Hans was an older champion saber fencer who had been Helene's mentor when she began her career at the Offenbach Fencing Club. They resumed their relationship and eventually he established his own studio. It became a prominent *salle d'arme* for serious fencers in the Bay Area.

Here was another avenue for Helene to whet her prodigious appetite. She was fencing as fast as she could! Throughout the war years, the *salle* also became a comforting place, a touch of home for Helene, as fencers gathered in Hans' small apartment behind the studio to gossip, drink beer, and relax after bouts. Sweating and spent, the fencers recalled the comradery, the close feelings they felt for one another. One fencer recalled "the beautiful dueling" between Helene and Hans.[15] Others called it "the glory days" at the Halberstadt Studio.

At the same time, Helene participated in demonstration matches at Stanford University and at the University of California, Berkeley. "One time her bra strap broke," stated a spectator at a Berkeley match. "Oops, there it goes," she said, and casually interrupted her match against Hans, fixing her bra strap in front of the audience. Grinning and provocative, she resumed play. Her sense of style and pacing added to the drama of the bouts. They were noisy affairs. She was called a "tigress," often grunting and crying out "Yes!" as she advanced toward her opponent. At Mills, Helene coached and choreographed fencing scenes for an all-girl student production of *Romeo and Juliet*.

At the end of the decade, with the world on the brink of a second world war, time passed agreeably enough in California. Helene now had three older men in her life—Dr. Blume, the head of the Mills' German Department whose task it was to see that she performed her teaching duties properly, Joe, and Hans.

It was Hans who understood her best. They shared potent memories of their childhoods in Offenbach and fencing at the club. Like Helene, Hans was the product of an assimilated family, perhaps as unconnected as she was to a Jewish identity.

The menace of Nazism loomed larger. World leaders acknowledged the threat and began to prepare for war against Germany. Growing awareness of a country gone mad forced the guardians of civilized behavior to take action.

The German occupation of Europe turned the continent into a perilous minefield from which few Jews and other refugees could escape. Many believed that the Nazi fixation on Jews would subside once Nazis faced the formidable power of the Allied response. They were wrong. In 1941, the transport of German Jews to death camps progressed. The "final solution"—extermination—was kept secret.

Mills College remained a shelter, a place of study for undergraduates who dutifully attended classes and earned their degrees. One student recalled, "I brought 10 evening dresses to Mills—I hardly wore them—there were no men around." Frivolous behavior was countered with concern about the war. Along with other members of the faculty, Dr. Blume made anti-Nazi speeches. Dr. Reinhardt, Mills' president, rescued Darius Milhaud, the famous French-Jewish composer who had escaped with his wife to England. President Reinhardt cabled Milhaud $500 toward his salary and the couple agreed to come to Mills, a college unknown to them.

Helene revealed to some students that she was partly Jewish. The Jewish designation was no longer a stinging embarrassment. Occasionally she "mentioned the persecution of the Jews in Germany . . . she did some soul searching" were comments of students who were on campus at that time. Helene continued to worry about her family's welfare. For four years, communication with Germany was severed and the usual correspondence between Helene and her family ceased. Her mother remained in Königstein. Trapped in Germany, both brothers managed to keep alive during the war years toiling as farm hands in Bavaria, and relying on helpful friends. Towards the end, as Germany's condition grew more desperate, Ludwig and Eugen survived in a specialized labor camp—it was their task to deport forced laborers to slave in mines where death awaited them. After the war, Ludwig made an unsuccessful attempt to immigrate to the United States. The two remained in Germany thereafter.

Although Helene rarely spoke of her past life, some students recalled seeing a photo of her wearing a sweater emblazoned with a swastika partially hidden by a towel. It disappeared. One student remembered Mademoiselle R who was head of the Mills French Department and hated Germans. "I was friendly with her and Helene. Mademoiselle R snubbed and avoided Helene. I discussed this with her and she agreed to approach mademoiselle. Helene won over the straight-laced French lady. I felt good about that."[16]

Helene played a small part in the war effort. After winning the U.S. National Women's Fencing title for the seventh time in 1942, she did not return to that competition in 1943. Instead, she undertook a special assignment in an army education project on the University of California, Berkeley campus to teach German to American servicemen who were going to be part of the occupation forces overseas. Men in her class had to learn a map of Berlin by heart; this was her exercise for them. In a message sent to the board of governors of the American Fencing League, she wrote, "The opportunity to assist in army education is more important at this time than fulfillment of purely personal interests."[17]

Helene back in her Mills College classroom
after winning the 1946 national women's foil title,
eliminating 13 opponents with 52 touches
while they scored seven

Chapter 14

THE FINAL CHAPTER

As war with Germany came to an end in May 1945, newspapers and radio revealed Nazi atrocities for the world to see. Much of European Jewry, 6 million in all, had been wiped out, along with their cultural history. Another 5 million people, outspoken Protestants and Catholics, gypsies, homosexuals, and the mentally or physically handicapped, had been exterminated for differing political or religious views or perceived physical or racial inferiority.

Helene's uncle, Georg August Mayer, a victim of Nazism, met his death in Theresienstadt in 1942 at the age of 62.[1] Her only remaining paternal relative, he had been sent to that concentration camp "reserved" for elderly Jews and those who had been wounded in World War I. It became a "model camp," the only one where the Nazis allowed foreign observers. Many of its inmates were prominent Jews whose final destination was to be Auschwitz, where death awaited them in the gas chamber.

Georg Mayer died before that final move.

The country Helene loved had come to an ignominious defeat. Germany had been to her the loveliest country of all, once beautiful, strong, and admired, now ugly, weak, and vilified. It was difficult for Helene to take pleasure in Germany's defeat and rejoice in the Allies' victory. She had defended it, suspending her own judgment for too long. Illusions about Germany received a deathblow as the reality took hold. The veneer of American citizenship eased the anguish and betrayal Helene felt as she confronted the most damning facts imaginable.

Communication with Helene's family had been impossible during the war years. A vexing worry, their living conditions were unknown to her. Afterward, she learned that her family had survived, but Helene did not immediately try to see them. Perhaps her hesitation stemmed from a need to protect herself from a startling encounter with the devastation inflicted on Germany. Perhaps she felt a sense of survivor guilt, contrasting her safe and secure spot in California with those who suffered the deprivations of war. It would have been unnerving to see the human and physical wreckage of her kin and her former country.

By the war's end, Helene's relationship to Mills College underwent a change. One student recalled that "she didn't seem to have loyal feelings towards Mills. If she got a job offer elsewhere, she would have left." She no longer gave intimate parties for "her girls" in her cottage. Perhaps she felt unable to quiet the prickly twinges of remorse. She may have been experiencing a restlessness and boredom with her predictable teaching duties. The war had taken its toll on her spirits. Immediately following the war, Dr. Blume and his family left Mills. Helene's relationship with Joe Sinel was faltering. One student said, "Helene desperately wanted to find the right guy and get married. She wanted a normal life." Helene was 35 years old and single and had reached an age when many athletes take a careful look at their future in sports.

Although some report that Helene didn't regret participating in the '36 Olympics, sometimes when asked if she had changed her mind she thoughtfully said *"nein."* But to others she offered revised remarks. During and after the war, students at Mills report that Helene said she "purposely lost" at the Olympics to defy the Nazi regime, to others she stated she was "forced to lose" after she was "pressured into competing." Many were aware of her discomfort—there was ambiguity and avoidance in reviewing the past.

But fencing was still a joy Helene could count on. Tournament play enhanced her life. In the summer of 1946, Helene won the U.S. National Women's Fencing title for the eighth and last time. An article in the *Oakland Tribune,* reiterating her fabled reputation, described her as "looking more like a glamorous fashion model than the greatest fencer in the world. . . . In her latest triumph, the German-born Miss Mayer outlasted 13 opponents in the recent New York City championships, with 52 touches while they scored 7." The article's headline, "Miss Mayer Set for '48 Games," looked to the resumption of the Olympic Games.

"If the United States were to send a women's foil fencing team to the 1948 Olympics," said Miss Mayer, "I believe it would have a very good chance to win the title." With her pleasant Austrian [*sic*] accent, Miss Mayer went on to explain that there has been no international competition since 1937. Since that time fencing in the country has taken great strides and the American women should do well, considering the sport has been neglected in war-torn Europe for the past seven years. As to the future competition, Miss Mayer . . . will compete under the flag of her adopted country or not at all. She would welcome the chance to take a crack at international competition.[2]

The resumption of the Olympic Games in 1948 heralded a return to international sports competition. London was chosen to be the host city for the first Games of the post–World War II era. For the second time in the 20th century, Germany was excluded from participation.

The magnetic pull of the Olympic Games whetted Helene's appetite for another try. Forget about the scars of war, politics, and nationalism. She was no longer a German citizen, she could represent her adopted country. If Helene were to fence in the 1948 Games, she had announced that she would do so as a naturalized American citizen. The challenge of confrontation, for the fourth time in her life in an Olympic setting, was her ultimate goal.

Unexpected upsets are often the lot of celebrity athletes. A surprising defeat dampened Helene's enthusiasm and weakened her resolve. The "foil queen" of American fencing lost her throne as the champion after eight consecutive years. She placed second in the 1947 tournament. It was a serious loss for an Olympics-bound athlete, by now unnerved by other troubles in her life. By this time, she and Joe Sinel had parted company, and the satisfactions of teaching at Mills College had diminished. The sustaining dream of fame and, possibly, fortune was rapidly fading.

"Life is not easy," wrote Helene to a friend in Germany in

1947. "I live in a country where everything is going much better than in Europe, but I have to slog away too, and don't live it up. I have two positions, in order to make ends meet—one at Mills College in the mornings and at the University of California in the afternoons and evenings . . . in the end you feel pretty much alone in this country."[3]

Helene revealed an unhappy state of mind and a shallow attachment to her adopted country. She was feeling lonely and dejected, and a note of self-pity clearly showed in her letter. When she returned to California following the 1947 tournament, she suddenly resigned from Mills to take a teaching position at San Francisco City College, a publicly funded school. She continued to live in her cottage near the Mills campus.

The 1947 women's foil fencing championship was Helene's last appearance in tournament play. Except for demonstration matches in the San Francisco area, she never fenced in major tournaments again. She was not a member of the American Olympics fencing team in 1948.

Helene's health began to deteriorate. Always in superb condition, she experienced sudden pain, weakness, and fatigue. It is unclear when breast cancer was diagnosed, but in 1948 she was feeling the initial symptoms of what was to become a terminal illness.

Helene made a visit home to Germany during the summer of 1948. Helene's brothers, Eugen and Ludwig, were alive. Ludwig had married in 1945, and Helene's mother still lived in Königstein. They were adjusting to an irrevocably changed Germany, partitioned into eastern and western zones where millions of sullen citizens, plagued by guilt and disbelief, rebuilt their lives. Once reassured of her family's safety, it was a depressing homecoming to a saddened and weary woman.

It was the year of the Summer Olympic games in London. At one time not so long ago, a trip to England would have been enticing and effortless for a world traveler and enthusiast like Helene. Now, demoralized and ill, she lost her zeal for combat and her taste for adventure. Although many in England grumbled that hosting the Games in 1948 was a waste of money that would have been better spent rebuilding their country, the Games went well and cheered the war-weary onlookers. Ironically, Ilona Schacherer-Elek, the 1936 gold medalist who never fenced against Helene again after 1937 in Paris, won the gold for the second time. Ellen Preis won the bronze again, and an American newcomer placed second. Helene did not attend.

Helene returned to California after her visit to Germany, still unaware of the tragic diagnosis awaiting her. Although she continued fencing intermittently at the Halberstadt studio, she was eventually forced to curtail her activities and endure multiple surgeries. In February 1952, she took a leave of absence without pay from City College to return to Germany for a "recuperative period."

Three months later, in May, she married a quintessential Bavarian, Baron Erwin Falkner von Sonnenburg, a structural engineer. A German acquaintance living in the United States acted as a go-between. The baron was described as a "fine, upstanding gentleman" by an American friend of Helene's. She and the baron lived in Heidelburg. Helene's earlier marked preference for tall men was no longer important. Her husband was shorter than she, but dignified in bearing. How he spent the war years was not revealed. Helene's penchant for attracting older, mature men who took on a protective role served her well. She was rescued from a frightening and financially troubling situation. Soon after her marriage the breast cancer metastasized to her spine.

In the summer of 1952, Helene was seriously ill. The Olympic Games that year were held in Helsinki, Finland. Ilona Schacherer-Elek, 45 years old, appeared to be on her way to another gold medal but was unexpectedly defeated by a Danish contender, Karen Lachmann.

Although her physical condition was worsening, Helene continued to take great interest in everything relating to fencing. In the summer of 1953, she received a visit from Hedwig Hass, a fencing "buddy" from the 1936 Olympics. Hass reported:

> She still wanted a full report about the world championship just completed in Brussels. Like me, for sixteen years she had not fenced with the greatest fencers of all countries and she was delighted when she heard a name that came to life again from the old times.[4]

Helene died on October 10, 1953, two months before her 43rd birthday. She was buried under a bed of flowers in the Wald cemetery in Munich in the family tomb of the Sonnenburg family.

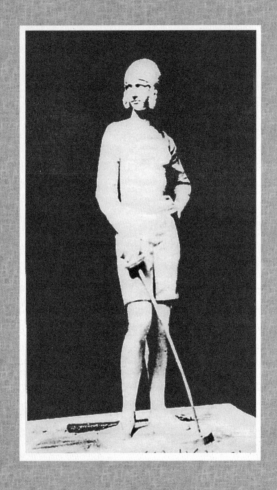

The plaster-of-Paris statuette
owned by thousands of German citizens
after the 1928 Olympic Games in Amsterdam

EPILOGUE

Erwin Casmir, Helene's long-time friend and fencing partner who had witnessed her performances in three Olympic Games (1928, 1932, and 1936) announced her death at a fencing championship tournament in Cologne, Germany. The Italian president of the International Fencing Federation dubbed her "the greatest champion of Amsterdam who opened the doors for women's fencing to all the international competitions." Her mother, Ida, thanked Mills College for funding a stipend in her name. She wrote, "It is indeed a comfort to know that my Helene was loved and admired by so many wonderful people." The Hans Halberstadt Fencing Club in San Francisco sponsored an annual tournament in Helene's honor, which drew hundreds of fencers to the Bay Area.

The well-wishers avoided mentioning her interaction with the Nazi regime, ignoring a past that had changed all their lives. It was a sad irony that Helene came by some to be viewed as a flawed opportunist and overzealous nationalist. Her memory would be stained by her refusal to take a prompt stand against the Nazi regime. The negotiations that Helene undertook to reinstate her once-esteemed position in Germany caused misgivings and led to uneasy feelings about her.

Now with the benefit of hindsight, we can perhaps better judge the implications of her negotiations surrounding the 1936 Games and their controversial outcome. Along with millions of others, Helene could not imagine the ultimate results of Nazi policies. Now that we know them, it is fitting to say that Helene's actions were disreputable. But from her point of view, what she had done to resurrect her standing was rational and understandable. As a celebrity and influential athlete, Helene was different but not so dissimilar from the rest of us who are pursued by urges of ambition and self-serving motives. It is no easy task to be fair in assessing Helene Mayer; she was often arrogant and blind to the ugly events around her.

Why was it so difficult for Helene to renounce Germany? In Helene's defense, it can be said that few people and governments envisioned such an end. Helene's steadfast allegiance and gratitude to the fatherland began when she was 13, an innocent, impressionable girl who had caught the public's eye and epitomized the perfection of her youth—a German youth. Yet naive in the ways of the world, Helene served her apprenticeship to the nation, blooming into a national phenomenon.

But in a period of rapid social change as the Nazis ascended, Helene's status was transformed. Her exalted position became a vulnerable one, subject to an arbitrary, capricious distinction that had no meaning to her—the Jewish label, an embarrassment, a mistake. While it is true that her father was Jewish, she had no ties to his heritage. She was essentially German in heart, mind, and body. As a result of relentless anti-Jewish propaganda, her image as the perfect German was fractured, torn apart by the irrefutable evidence of her "tainted" blood. She shunned the repugnant distinction, believing that no government, even a nasty one, could sever her connection with Germany. The contract had been sealed in her youth.

She believed herself to be a quintessential German. Her decisions were motivated by a dogged adherence to her "German-ness," belonging to one culture and one people. The deeply entrenched commitment shaped her part in the Olympic controversy.

Helene played a crucial role in ensuring that the 1936 Games would go forward. Her behavior was driven by a belief in herself as an athlete and a German whose good name had been sorely compromised. The Games provided the setting for Helene to make a comeback, to restore those little statues of the Golden "He" that had been tossed into the trash or hidden away in dusty attics by a dwindling number of admirers.

In this moral drama, world opinion was heavily weighted in favor of participation. Those who would boycott the Olympics fought a losing battle, unable to overcome the powerful groups that were prepared to go to Berlin despite the betrayals of the Nazi regime. To the great relief of Olympic planners and power brokers, Helene finally agreed to bear the designation of Jew. It was her price of admission. If she had taken steps on behalf of those Germans whom the Nazis were punishing, if she chose to protest, she would have acted in a way that would have imperiled her two most critical goals—to perform as an athlete in the Olympics and to be reinstated as a German citizen. In a woeful display of compromised behavior, she bargained carefully to have her citizenship restored.

History is not pre-ordained. What if the Olympic committees had refused to ignore Nazi outrages against German-Jewish athletes? What if Helene had refused to allow herself to be the "token Jew" and had not indulged in wishful thinking entering into negotiations with the Nazis? Would a show of moral indignation and refusal to haggle with a corrupt regime have slowed the pace or forced the Nazis to control their murderous inclinations? "What if" questions reasonably raise the issue of individual and collective decisions that can have a profound effect on altering history.

In comparison to the machinations and bargaining during the Olympic controversy, the image of Helene's Nazi salute at the medals awards ceremony was of a lesser consequence, although in later years it assumed infamous symbolic importance. In 1936, the "Heil Hitler" salute was both a provocative, discomfiting gesture to some and to supporters it was a gesture of admiration for Hitler and his charismatic leadership. Once Helene became a member of the 1936 German Olympic team and a silver medal winner, her salute was a "hurrah" to cheering crowds and dignitaries, including Hitler. It was her proclamation of fidelity. As Nazi intransigence gave way to brutality, the salute came to epitomize allegiance to a crazed, criminal despot. In 1936, his horrific reputation was not yet enshrined in the minds of the public.

By 1936, the Olympic Games had become a prestigious, coveted setting for the most rigorously trained amateur athletes in the world. Most worthy athletes were eager to follow the Olympic torch to any host country. In these Games, rivalry ruled the play; the theme of international harmony was diminished. The Games were about power, dominance, and strident nationalism. George Orwell, author of *1984,* observed in 1945 after Germany's defeat:

> Sport is an unfailing cause of ill will because it is bound up with the rise of nationalism—the lunatic modern habit of identifying oneself with large power units and seeing everything in terms of competitive prestige.

Avery Brundage, the hypocritical president of the American Olympic Committee, made the falsely reassuring point in regard to the Olympics: "Here there is no injustice of caste, of race, of family, of wealth." If only this was so. Helene and all the other athletes had to shut out the controversies that swirled around them. They had two goals: to honor a national connection and to exhibit their unique skills.

Athletes, like ordinary citizens, are often disinclined to enter the political arena. Politics is a complicated and messy business of lesser concern to those who yearn for the opportunity at fame and perhaps a chance to become an enduring figure in sports history. Much is at stake. Tunnel vision and focused ambition can undermine the development of moral concerns. Each athlete is partially governed by rules and policies laid down by layers of decision makers—governments, the IOC, the national Olympic committees, specific athletic organizations, coaches—whose oftentimes controversial decisions raised huge questions in the Games.

The Olympic athletes faced the same moral dilemmas Helene faced. When are moral boundaries breached? At what point does any individual, a single athlete, stand alone to denounce unfairness? What are the constraints on an athlete speaking out when his or her career, or perhaps life, is at stake? In the Games, the facts speak for themselves. Despite a powerful boycott movement, the United States as a pivotal player came close to bowing out. But in the end, 4,000 athletes participated, obscuring those athletes who withdrew.

In the journey to the 1936 Olympics, opponents of fascism who would not stop insisting on its dangers, had their say. Judge Mahoney, the embattled president of the Amateur Athletic Union; William Shirer, the prophetic historian and journalist; John Lardner and other thoughtful journalists; a small group of athletes; and the anonymous few people who placed boycott material in the cabins of American athletes, skewering the Nazis and attempting to arouse the public. The boycotters grasped the wider implication of participation in the Nazi Olympics. Their warnings fell on deaf ears. The Games acted as a magnet, irresistibly drawing athletes and sports fans to it.

Helene's story is one of an individual in a time that transformed and tested the human experience. Based on her formative years in Germany, Helene had to make judgments, act on her decisions, and cope with the consequences of her choices. Imagine the monumental task for any individual caught in the complex entanglement of human nature and the outside forces of time, place, and happenstance. What began as a love affair with her homeland soured. Germany had been the suitor, Helene the once adored. The relationship turned into a demoralized pursuit of a suitor gone mad. In Helene's eyes, she had done nothing wrong; the rejection was confounding. When Helene was declared a Jew, the new ideology swept away her athletic prowess, her marvelous blonde beauty, her loyalty, and her deserved fame. Try as she might, she could not woo the lover back. Caught in the clutches of Nazism, her beloved had turned into a beast, hellbent on redefining the nature of a human being. The Nazi State would have the supreme right to decide who was worthy of love and who could live, and who was unworthy and had to die.

The quandary between self-interest and the common good is played out in this narrative about Helene Mayer. We remember the heroic figures who argued on behalf of humanity. They stand for the best in us. But we also acknowledge the worst in ourselves, like Helene, clinging to shortsighted self-protective behaviors. The poignant words of the Jewish philosopher and sage Hillel are fitting. They go to the "I"—the individual, Helene—who had to make the hard choices. He wrote, "If I am not for myself, who am I? If I am only for myself, what am I? If not now, when?" These questions go to the heart of the matter. Had Helene been capable of asking herself these questions, she might have acted differently. Could she have found a way of reconciling her self-interest and the moral imperatives of taking a stand against the Nazi regime?

A final vision of Helene leaves her on a dimly lit stage. She is wearing a pristine fencing costume, immaculately white. Her hair is carefully in place under her wire mask. Her foil is in position. Her opponents appear one by one as they move forward from the shadows. Cavaliere Gazzera, her childhood instructor at the Offenbach Fencing Club, is first. Innocent and eager, she parries with him. The jousting is gentle, like a ballet. He is the teacher, she the respected student.

Another loving figure, her father, Ludwig Mayer, appears, foil in hand. He encourages her to lunge, to reach out, and engage him in a mock duel. Does she try to wound the father figure or run from it?

She fences gaily and teasingly with a Mills College student. Now she displays her skill and prowess to her student.

Helene enters into a pitiful encounter with the stereotypic Jew, clumsy, overdressed, inept. He is hardly an adversary. Her Jewish mantle becomes prominent and unwanted; does it conceal her fencing costume, dragging her down by its weight?

Helene maintains her self-control and faces the contest with a Nazi, who could be Tschammer und Osten, the Nazi sports minister. Helene is on guard; he lunges, she backs off. She has to plan her moves carefully.

Another opponent appears. Perhaps it is Reinhard Heydrich, the "Blonde Beast." He makes an offensive thrust. She parries in return, deflecting his hit. He is stronger and shows no mercy. Helene has few opportunities for a riposte, but she does manage one successful hit to his torso. Enraged, her opponent abandons the rules of engagement and lunges toward her head, legs, all the vulnerable spots until he hits her heart, a mocking, seductive smile on his lips. Exhausted, Helene makes a final thrust but she cannot strike a winning blow.

The final contender is a woman. She resembles Ilona Schacherer-Elek, Helene's opponent at the 1936 Olympics. Does Helene see the irony in the fact that Ilona is also a half-Jew although they have little in common beside their fencing ability? Helene loses confidence and despite her best efforts, she is defeated.

One by one, the opponents disappear. Helene removes her mask and drops her foil soundlessly. She is neither victor nor loser, just another voyager forlorn and detached from the heat of competition. The contests have sapped her strength. What began as brilliant promise in Offenbach has ended with loss and ambiguity in Berlin. Helene feels very tired. It has been a long journey.

Postscript

The German post office in 1968 issued a series of special Olympic stamps, honoring great figures that had enhanced the Games. Pierre de Coubertin, the founder of the modern Games, was honored as was Carl von Langen, a popular horseman and winner in the Amsterdam Games in 1928. Carl Diem, the sports educator who planned the athletic events at the 1936 Games, was honored as well as Rudolf Harbig, the world champion in the 400-meter race. Only one woman was honored. It was Helene Mayer, her youthful profile etched on a rosy pink postage stamp.

Sports Illustrated, the noted sports magazine, listed Helene Mayer as one of the 100 greatest female athletes of the 20th century. She was ranked 83rd in the 1999-2000 *Sports Illustrated for Women* issue. Athletes were selected by representatives of the magazine(s)—CNN/SI, editors, writers, and correspondents who considered the athlete's onfield performance and achievements, plus their contributions to women's sports.

Helene Mayer Chronology

12/10/1910	Helene Mayer born in Offenbach, Germany
1914–1918	World War I
1919	Treaty of Versailles
1920	Helene begins fencing
1923	Helene, age 13, wins German National Championship
	Adolph Hitler's "Beer Hall Putsch"
1925	Paul von Hindenburg elected President of Germany
1928	Germany re-enters Olympic Games
	Helene wins gold medal in Amsterdam
1929	European World Champion
1930	Helene graduates Schillerschule, Frankfurt, with honors
	European World Champion
	Enters University of Frankfurt
1931	One semester at Sorbonne, Paris
	European World Champion
	Death of Helene's father, Dr. Ludwig Mayer
1932	Exchange student at Scripps College, Claremont, California

1932	Places fifth at Olympic Games in Los Angeles
	Deepening economic depression in United States
	Franklin D. Roosevelt elected president
1933	Adolph Hitler named chancellor of Germany
	National boycott and restrictions on Jewish businesses and professionals, including athletes
	Helene continues education at Scripps College
	Expelled in absentia from Offenbach Fencing Club
	Exchange student status rescinded by Nazi regime
	United States National Champion
1934	Helene completes masters program at Scripps College
	Accepts teaching and fencing position at Mills College, Oakland, California
	United States National Champion
1935	Death of President von Hindenburg
	Germany reoccupies the Rhineland in violation of the Treaty of Versailles
	Passage of Nuremberg Laws rescinding citizenship of Jewish Germans
	Helene continues teaching German and fencing at Mills College
	United States National Champion
1936	Berlin Olympic Games
	Helene wins silver medal (second place)
	Continues teaching at Mills College
1937	Wins World Championship, Paris
	Wins United States National Championship
	Participates in Canadian exhibition matches on return to Mills

1938	Germany occupies and partitions Czechoslovakia
	Nazi regime initiates *Kristallnacht* (night of glass), systematically destroying synagogues and Jewish businesses throughout Germany
	United States National Champion
1939	Germany invades Poland, causing declaration of war by England and France
1940	Fall of France
	Helene becomes American citizen
	United States National Champion
1941	United States declares war against Japan and Germany
	United States National Champion
1942	United States National Champion
1943	Helene teaches languages to American soldiers at University of California, Berkeley
	Helene decides not to compete in United States National Fencing Tournament
1944	World War II continues
1945	Germany surrenders to Allied Forces
	Hitler commits suicide
	United Nations created in San Francisco
1946	Helene wins United States National Championship for last time
1947	Helene resigns abruptly from Mills College, takes position at City College, San Francisco
	Places second in United States National Fencing Tournament
1948	Resumption of Olympic Games in London
	Helene does not participate; possible onset of cancer

1949–1950	Helene teaches at City College
1951	Fencing at Hans Halberstadt Studio
1952	Returns to Germany
	Marries Baron Erwin Falker von Sonnenburg
10/10/1953	Helene dies of cancer two months before her 43rd birthday
	Buried in Munich, Germany

Endnotes

Chapter 1: The Golden He

1. Jonas W. Klaus, "Eine Ausserordentliche Personliche Keit: Zur Erinnerung An Helene Mayer (20.12.1910—15.10.1953)" ("An Extraordinary Person: In Memory of Helene Mayer"), *Fechtsport,* June 1982, p. 8.

2. Von Hans-Joachim Leyenberg, "Offenbachs 'blonde He': Olympiasiegerin und KronzEugen eines deutschen Schicksals" ("Offenbachs 'blonde He': Olympic Winner and Main Witness of a German Fate"), *Frankfurter Allgemeine,* December 24, 1993, p. 56.

3. Ibid.

4. Ruth Gay, *Jews of Germany—A Historical Portrait,* p. xi and p. 161.

5. Ibid., p. 249.

6. Ibid., p. 253.

Chapter 2: The Olympics before 1928

1. Quoted in Leyenberg, *Frankfurter Allgemeine,* December 24, 1993, p. 56.

2. Jennifer Hargreaves, "Women and the Olympic Phenomenon," *Five Ring Circus—Money, Power and Politics at the Olympic Games,* ed. A. Tomlinson and G. Uhannel, p. 54.

3. Adrianne Blue, *Faster, Higher, Further—Women's Triumphs and Disasters at the Olympics,* p. 3.

ENDNOTES

4. William O. Johnson, *The Olympics, A History of the Games*, p. 13.
5. Ibid., p. 18.
6. Jennifer Hargreaves, "Women and the Olympic Phenomenon," in *Five Ring Circus*, p. 57.
7. Johnson, *The Olympics, A History of the Games*, p. 35.

Chapter 3: The Jewish Legacy
1. Gay, *Jews of Germany*, p. 4.
2. *Encyclopedia Judaica*.
3. Ibid., p. 2.
4. Ibid., p. 3.
5. Gay, *Jews of Germany*, p. 22.
6. Stadtarchiv Mainz (city archive), Mayer family tree supplied by city archivist Frau Braun.
7. Daniel Goldhagen, *Hitler's Willing Executioners*, p. 64.
8. Lucy S. Dawidowicz, *The War Against the Jews, 1933-1945*, p. 43-44.
9. Quote from an obituary in Mainz newspaper at time of Martin Mayer's death, April 26, 1917, from city archive, Mainz.

Chapter 4: The Early Years in Offenbach
1. Gay, *Jews of Germany*, p. 182.
2. *Encyclopedia Judaica*, CD-ROM Edition.
3. "Zur Geschichter der Juden in Offenbach am Main" ("The History of Jews in Offenbach am Main"), *Band 2*, Stadtarchiv (city archive), pp. 212-214.
4. Ibid.
5. *Offenbach Zeitung* (quote from obituary re: Dr. Ludwig Mayer), Stadtarchiv (city archive), April 28, 1931.
6. Recollection of Margaret Graham, February 2, 1998.
7. Frank Menke and Peter Palmer, *Encyclopedia of Sports*, p. 364.
8. *Encyclopedia Americana*, Vol. II, 1999. p. 92.
9. Gay, *Jews of Germany*, p. 212.

10. Ibid., p. 212.
11. Gertrude Pfister and Toni Niewerth, "Jewish Women in Gymnastics and Sport in Germany, 1898-1938," *Journal of Sports History,* Volume 26, Summer 1999, p. 315.
12. Klaus, *Fechtsport Magazine,* p. 8.
13. Leyenberg, *Frankfurter Allgemeine,* p. 56.
14. Dawidowicz, *The War Against the Jews,* p. 22.
15. Ibid., p. 23.

Chapter 5: The Schillerschule Years

1. Klaus, *Fechtsport,* p. 8.
2. Dr. Mayer's letter dated October 20, 1921, in *Denkmal* (Memorial), historical document prepared by six graduates of Schillerschule, February 1993, p. 5.
3. Pfister and Niewerth, *Journal of Sports History,* p. 315.
4. Klaus, *Fechtsport,* p. 8.
5. Ibid.
6. Ibid.
7. *Denkmal,* Schillerschule, p. 6.
8. Ibid.
9. Ibid.
10. Klaus, *Fechtsport,* p. 9.
11. Leyenberg, *Frankfurter Allgemeine,* p. 56.
12. *The Holocaust,* Holocaust Exhibition at the Imperial War Museum, London, June 2000, p. 12.
13. Dawidowicz, *The War Against the Jews,* p. 23.
14. Time-Life Books, *Storming to Power,* The Third Reich Series, p. 36.

Chapter 6: A Life Interrupted

1. Klaus, *Fechtsport,* p. 9.
2. Time-Life Books, *Storming to Power,* p. 78.
3. *Offenbach Zeitung* (quote from obituary re: Dr. Ludwig Mayer. Stadtarchiv (city archive), April 28, 1931. Mr. Hans Ruppel, city

archivist, noted that Martha Wertheimer composed the obituary. She worked for many years as an editor for the *Offenbach* [1919-1933] and took her own life in 1942 when she was about to be transported to Auschwitz.).

4. *Denkmal*, p. 19.

5. Leyenberg, *Frankfurter Allgemeine,* December 24, 1993, p. 56.

6. Recollection of Becky Bacon Buddhue, February 5, 1998.

7. *Scripps College—A Resident College for Women,* 1933.

8. Dawidowicz, *The War Against the Jews,* pp. 66-67.

9. Recollection of Becky Bacon Buddhue, February 5, 1998.

10. Time-Life Books, *The New Order,* p. 59.

11. Dawidowicz, *The War Against the Jews,* p. 67.

12. Gay, *Jews of Germany,* p. 255.

13. Dawidowicz, *The War Against the Jews,* p. 84.

14. Valentin Senger, *No. 12, Kaiserhofstrasse, The Story of an Invisible Jew in Nazi Germany,* p. 72.

15. Ibid., p. 20.

16. Recollection of Katherine Zimmerman, February 2, 1998.

17. Leyenberg, *Frankfurter Allgemeine,* December 24, 1993, p. 56.

18. Gay, *Jews of Germany,* p. 257.

19. Duff-Hart Davis, *Hitler's Games—The 1936 Olympics,* p. 63.

20. *Scripture,* October 23, 1934, p. 2.

Chapter 7: Mills College

1. Recollection of Isabelle Wiel, February 4, 1998.

2. Time-Life Books, *The New Order,* pp. 46-47.

3. Deutsches Marine Institute Archives (German Naval Archives), re: Captain Lütjens and voyage of training warship, *Karlsruhe III.*

4. *Mills College Weekly,* February 12, 1935, p. 1.

5. Tinka Strauss, *Mills College Weekly,* "Labor Camps for Women in Germany," May 30, 1935.

6. Dawidowicz, *The War Against the Jews,* pp. 87-89.

7. Ibid., p. 91.

Chapter 8: The Olympics Controversy

1. Allen Guttmann, *The Olympics*, p. 53.
2. Richard Mandell, *The Nazi Olympics*, New York, 1971, p. 39.
3. Ibid., p. 54.
4. Ibid., p. 55.
5. David B. Kanin, *Political History of the Olympic Games*, p. 54.
6. Ibid., p. 53.
7. *American Hebrew*, New York, November 2, 1935.
8. Guttmann, *The Olympics*, p. 57.
9. Marta Glazer, "Corruption of the Olympic Ideal: 1936 and 1972" (Senior thesis, University of Pennsylvania, 1997), p. 20.
10. Ibid., p. 28.
11. Ibid., p. 26.
12. Guttmann, *The Olympics*, p. 60.
13. *American Hebrew*, "American Press Comments on the Olympics," November 8, 1935, pp. 41-43.
14. *American Hebrew*, last section of Mahoney's letter to Lewald, October 25, 1935.
15. Guttmann, *The Olympics*, p. 65.
16. Nederland Olympisch Comite (Netherlands Olympic Committee), received from R. D. Paauw, August 26, 1998.
17. *New York Times* obituary, "Ruth Langer Lawrence, 77, Who Boycotted the '36 Olympics," June 6, 1999.

Chapter 9: Helene in the Spotlight

1. *New York Times*, "Miss Mayer, Noted Fencing Star, Here From Coast in Quest of U.S. Title," April 10, 1934.
2. Heywood Broun, Scripps-Howard newspaper, reprinted in *Hebrew Weekly*, "Public Against Olympics," August 23, 1935.
3. *New York Times*, "German Sports Chief to Make Plea Here," September 26, 1935.
4. Jahnke's letter to Lewald, reprinted in *American Hebrew*, October

25, 1935.

5. *New York Times*, "Dr. Lewald Calls Mahoney Meddler," October 26, 1935.

6. *American Hebrew*, "Interpretations of Current Events—Stage Cleared for Olympics Showdown," November 1, 1935.

7. Politisches Archiv Des Auswartigen Amts (Political Archive of the Office of Foreign Affairs), Band R' 9873.

8. Ibid.

9. Ibid.

10. Arnd Krüger, *Die Olympischen Spiele, 1936 und die Weltmeinung*, (*The Olympic Games of 1936 and Public Opinion*), p. 131.

11. Ibid.

12. Mandell, *The Nazi Olympics*, p. 93.

13. Frederick T. Birchall, *New York Times*, "Olympics Begin Today in Germany," February 6, 1936.

14. *New York Times*, "Miss Mayer Departs," February 13, 1936.

15. *New York Times*, "Miss Mayer in Tryouts," February 20, 1936.

16. *Denkmal*, p. 49.

Chapter 10: The Nazi Olympiad—1936

1. Klaus, *Fechtsport*, p. 9.

2. Mandell, *The Nazi Olympics*, p. 122.

3. Ibid., p. 126.

4. Ibid., p. 136.

5. Davis, *Hitler's Games*, p. 155.

6. Ibid., pp. 157-158.

7. Lewis H. Carlson and John J. Fogarty, *Tales of Gold—An Oral History of the Summer Olympic Games*, pp. 137-138.

Chapter 11: Helene and the Games

1. William L. Shirer, *The Rise and Fall of the Third Reich*, pp. 232-233.

2. Mandell, *The Nazi Olympics*, p. 140.

3. Collections du Musée Olympique (Collections of the Olympic Museum), The Gods of the Stadium Exhibit, the role of the news media in Olympic Games, Paris, June 2001.
4. Carlson and Fogarty, *Tales of Gold,* pp. 187-188.
5. William O. Johnson, *All That Glitters is Not Gold,* p. 36.
6. Carlson and Fogarty, *Tales of Gold,* p. 140.
7. Mandell, *The Nazi Olympics,* p. 181.
8. Adrianne Blue, *Faster, Higher, Further—Women's Triumphs and Disasters at the Olympics,* pp. 44-45.
9. Mandell, *The Nazi Olympics,* p. 182.
10. Nick Evangelista, *Encyclopedia of the Sword,* p. 386.
11. Carlson and Fogarty, *Tales of Gold,* pp. 83-84.
12. Exhibit at the Olympic Museum, Paris, June 2001.
13. Carlson and Fogarty, *Tales of Gold,* pp. 141-142.
14. Ibid., p. 90.
15. *Denkmal,* p. 65.

Chapter 12: The Olympic Pause

1. Glazier, "Corruption of the Olympic Ideal," p. 59.
2. Carlson and Fogarty, *Tales of Gold,* p. 154.
3. Ibid., p. 174.
4. Ibid., p. 181.
5. Charles Lawliss, . . . *and God Cried—The Holocaust Remembered,* p. 42.
6. Mandell, *The Nazi Olympics,* p. 92.
7. *Mills College Weekly,* October 26, 1936.
8. Recollection of Francis Sohn, September 14, 1997.
9. "Die Blonde Hee," *Freitag,* No. 31, July 28, 1961, p. 14.

Chapter 13: A Doomed Decade

1. *Frankfurter Allgemeine,* December 24, 1993, p. 56.
2. Recollection of Margaret Graham, January 29, 1993.
3. Dawidowicz, *The War Against the Jews,* p. 130.

4. Recollection of Gertrude Gibbs, April 29, 1998.

5. *Arthur Lane Remembers Helene Mayer, 1936-1953*, p. 8.

6. Ibid.

7. Ibid., p. 9.

8. Dawidowicz, *The War Against the Jews*, p. 103.

9. Christoph Amberger, "Sabres and Swastikas," *American Fencing*, Summer 1995, Volume 45, p. 18.

10. Read and Fisher, *Kristallnacht*, p. 29.

11. Dawidowicz, *The War Against the Jews*, pp. 141-142.

12. Interview with Rondal Partridge, February 15, 1998.

13. Edan Milton Hughes, *Artists in California, 1786-1940*, Meyer Library, California College of Arts and Crafts, California, p. 517.

14. Lawliss, . . . *and God Cried—The Holocaust Remembered*, p. 18.

15. Recollection of Mary "Demi" Huddleson, September 25, 1997.

16. Recollection of Marion Doty, January 14, 1998.

17. *Mills College, Today and Tomorrow*, June 1943.

Chapter 14: The Final Chapter

1. Stadtarchiv, Mainz.

2. Charley MacIntosh, *Oakland Tribune*, July 7. 1948.

3. Klaus, *Fechtsport*, June 1982, p. 10.

4. Ibid., p. 10.

Bibliography

Books

Anissimov, Myriam. *Primo Levi—Tragedy of an Optimist*. Woodstock, New York: Overlook Press, 1999.

Blue, Adrianne. *Faster, Higher, Further—Women's Triumphs and Disasters at the Olympics*. London: Virago Press Ltd., 1988.

Carlson, Lewis H. and John J. Fogarty. *Tales of Gold—An Oral History of the Summer Olympic Games Told by America's Gold Medal Winners*. Chicago: Contemporary Books, 1987.

Davis, Duff-Hart. *Hitler's Games—The 1936 Olympics*. London: Century Hutchinson Ltd., 1987.

Dawidowicz, Lucy S. *The War Against the Jews, 1933-1945*. New York: Bantam Books, 1981.

Denkmal (memorial) to Helene Mayer, written by graduates of the Schillerschule, published by Gioeschichts-Agder Schillerschule (1993).

Dunn, L. C. *A Short History of Genetics*. Ames: Iowa State University Press, 1991.

Gay, Ruth. *Jews of Germany—A Historical Portrait*. New Haven, Connecticut: Yale University Press, 1992.

Goldhagen, Daniel J. *Hitler's Willing Executioners—Ordinary Germans and the Holocaust*. New York: Knopf, 1996.

Guttmann, Allen. *The Olympics—A History of the Modern Games*.

BIBLIOGRAPHY

Urbana: University of Illinois Press, 1992.

Johnson, William O. *All That Glitters Is Not Gold: The Olympic Game.* New York: Putnam, 1972.

Johnson, William O. *The Olympics: A History of the Games.* New York: Bishop Books, Inc., 1992.

Kanin, David B. *Political History of the Olympic Games.* Boulder, Colorado: Westview Press, 1981.

Krüger, Arnd. *Die Olympischen Spiele, 1936 und die Weltmeinung (The Olympic Games of 1936 and Public Opinion).* Berlin: Verlag, Bartels and Wernitz, 1972.

Lawliss, Charles. *. . . and God Cried—The Holocaust Remembered.* New York: JG Press, 1994.

Lipstadt, Deborah E. *Beyond Belief—The American Press and the Coming of the Holocaust, 1933-1945.* New York: Free Press, 1986.

Mandell, Richard D. *The Nazi Olympics.* New York: Macmillan, 1971.

Preis, Ellen. *Olympiaseig.* Vienna: Payer & Co., 1936.

Read, Anthony and David Fisher. *Kristallnacht: The Nazi Night of Terror.* New York: Random House, 1989.

Schaap, Dick. *An Illustrated History of the Olympics.* New York: Knopf, 1975.

Senger, Valentin. *No. 12, Kaiserhofstrasse—The Story of an Invisible Jew in Nazi Germany.* New York City: Dutton, 1980.

Shirer, William L. *The Rise and Fall of the Third Reich.* New York: Simon and Schuster, 1959.

Time-Life Editors. *The Third Reich: The Twisted Dream, The Center of the Web, Storming to Power.* Alexandria, Virginia: Time-Life Books, Inc., 1989.

Tomlinson, Alan and Gary Whannel. *Five Ring Circus—Money, Power and Politics at the Olympic Games.* London: Pluto Press, 1984.

Wallechinsky, David. *The Complete Book of the Olympics.* New York: Little, Brown and Co., 1992.

Periodicals

Amberger, Christoph J., "Sabres and Swastikas," *American Fencing,* volume 45, no.2 (Summer 1995).

DeCapriles, Mignes, "Helene Mayer (1910-1953)," obituary, *American Fencing,* no. 2 (December, 1953).

Diem, Karl, "Women in Sports in Modern Germany," *Sportswoman,* volume 8, no. 5 (January 1932).

Eisen, George, "Jewish History and the Ideology of Modern Sport," *Approaches and Interpretations* (Fall 1998).

Klaus, Jonas W., "Eine Ausserordent liche Personlichkeit" (An Extraordinary Personality), in memory of Helene Mayer, *Fechtsport* (June 1982).

Krüger, Arnd, "Fair Play for American Athletes—A Study in Anti-Semitism," *Canadian Journal of Sports and Physical Education* (May, 1978).

Leyenberg, Von Hans-Joachim, "Offenbach's 'blonde He': Olympiasiegerin und KronzEugen eines deutschen Schicksals" ("Offenbach's 'blonde He,' Olympic Winner and Main Witness of a German Fate"), *Frankfurter Allgemeine* (December 24, 1993).

Pfister, Gertrude and Toni Nieworth, "Jewish Women in Gymnastics and Sport in Germany, 1898-1938," *Journal of Sports History*, volume 26, no. 2 (Summer 1999).

Archives

American

American Jewish Archives, Cincinnati, Ohio. Microfilm copies of *American Hebrew* and *Jewish Tribune* (1935-36).

Leo Baeck Institute, New York City. Devoted to research of German-speaking Jews from the Enlightenment to the Holocaust.

German

Stadtarchiv, Mainz.

Stadtarchiv, Offenbach.

Deutsche Fechter Bund (German Fencing Society), Bund.

Deutsche Marine Institut (German Naval Institute), re: training ship *Karlsrune III* in San Francisco Port (February, 1935).

Politisches Archiv Des Auswartigen AMTS (Political Archive of the Office of Foreign Affairs).

Israeli

Wingate Institute, Netanya, Israel.

Oral History

Arthur Lane Remembers Helene Mayer, 1936-1953. Oral history. Interview conducted by Kristen Harber, 1992, Bancroft Library, University of California, Berkeley. (1992)

Senior Thesis

Glazier, Marta. "Corruption of the Olympic Ideal: 1936 and 1972," Senior thesis, University of Pennsylvania, 1997.

Newspapers

American
Los Angeles Register
Mills College Weekly
New York Times
Oakland Tribune
San Francisco Chronicle
Scripture

German
Frankfurter Allgemeine
Freitag
Der Tagesspiegel
Zeit

Museums

Holocaust Memorial Museum, Washington, D. C.
Imperial War Museum, London
Judisches Museum, Frankfurt
Judah Magnes Museum, Berkeley, California
Musee Olympique, Paris
National Olympic Museum, Frankfurt
Olympic Museum, Lausanne, Switzerland

Encyclopedias

Encyclopedia Americana. Danbury, Connecticut: Grolier, 1999.
Encyclopedia of the Sword. Nick Evangelista. Westport, Connecticut: Greenwood Press, 1995.

Acknowledgments

MANY THANKS to the Mills College Alumnae Association and those former students who shared their recollections of Helene Mayer: Marion Sanborn Doty, Billie Dunfee, Leona Evans, Gertrude E. Gibbs, Margaret Graham, Francis Smyrl Jennings, Jane Kenyon, Genevieve Whitmore King, Francis Sohn, Jane Tucker, Isabelle Wiel, and Ann Salzburger Wolff.

Thanks to Frank Blume and Rondal Partridge who had vivid recollections of Mills.

Becky Bacon Buddhue and Katherine Zimmerman met Helene at Scripps College and spoke of their long-lasting relationship with her.

Fencing "buddies" Tommy Angell and Mary "Demi" Huddleson also supplied relevant information.

Arthur Lane, a San Francisco Bay Area fencing master, and Andy Shaw, fencing historian, were most helpful.

Judy Harvey Sahak, director of Dennison Library, Scripps College, and Janet Braun, Special Collections Curator at Olin Library, Mills College, provided generous support. Thanks too to the library staff at the North Berkeley branch of the Berkeley Public Library.

Former Vice Consul Joachim Cordes at the German Consulate in San Francisco was emphatically helpful, as were Hans G. Ruppel, archivist of the city of Offenbach, and Frau Braun, archivist of the city of Mainz.

Margaret Lambert, neé Gretel Bergmann, and Erika Mayer, Helene's sister-in-law, shared important details.

Doris Runzheimer of Hamburg, Germany, generously made available her recollections of and letters from Helene.

Thanks to Julia Koch for her unstinting help as a translator.

I am grateful to Linda Polsby, Bob Drews, and Kim Klescewski for their editing skills.

Thanks to Carol Levy for her research assistance.

Mel, you lent a sustaining, firm hand! Many thanks!

—Milly Mogulof

Index

INDEX

Photo Credits

Page viii: Courtesy of Mary "Demi" Huddleson

Page 16: Courtesy of Mary "Demi" Huddleson

Page 26: *Mills Quarterly,* Fall 1999

Page 38: Courtesy of *Denk mal* (Memorial)

Page 76: Courtesy of Mary "Demi" Huddleson

Page 134: Courtesy of *Denk mal*

Page 138: Library of Congress, from *IX Olympiade, Berlin, 1936*

Page 142: From *An Illustrated History of the Olympics,* 2nd Edition, Dick Schaap, 1963, 1967

Page 148: Courtesy of Mary "Demi" Huddleson

Page 156: Courtesy of Mary "Demi" Huddleson

Page 168: Courtesy of Mary "Demi" Huddleson

Page 210: *Oakland Tribune,* July 7, 1946, no. 7

Page 218: Courtesy of Mary "Demi" Huddleson

Page 253: Courtesy of David Gahr

About the Author

Milly Mogulof grew up in Brooklyn, New York, at the time the Nazis came to power in Germany. She received her undergraduate and graduate education at Brooklyn College, the University of Pennsylvania and the University of California, Berkeley. She became interested in the life story of Helene Mayer while working as a mental health professional in the Bay Area.